FESTO KIVENGERE

Map of Uganda
showing Anglican dioceses (1984)

FESTO
KIVENGERE

Frank Retief

EP PUBLISHING WITH A MISSION

EP BOOKS
Faverdale North
Darlington, DL3 0PH
England

web: http://www.epbooks.org

e-mail: sales@epbooks.org

First published 2012

British Library Cataloguing in Publication Data available

ISBN: 978-0-85234-851-2

Printed and bound in Great Britain by MPG Books Group, Bodmin and King's Lynn.

CONTENTS

Acknowledgements

I need to express my great debt to several people for assisting me with this little book.

Anne Coomes
Anne is Festo Kivengere's official biographer. Her extensive and well-researched work formed the platform for this book. She kindly read my manuscript and gave me permission to use her work and to quote her extensively.

Dawn Clulow
Dawn is a PA to the Church of England in South Africa's Administrative Office in Cape Town. My own secretary was ill during the writing of this book and Dawn took over my work, adding to her already heavy programme.

Michael Cassidy
Michael is the founder of Africa Enterprise. He is a well-known and very gifted evangelist. Michael is respected all over Africa and the rest of the world, not only for his

evangelistic work but also because of his untiring work for reconciliation especially during South Africa's apartheid years. He is a visionary leader and the organization he founded has impacted large sections of Africa and other parts of the world. His relationship with Festo was well known. Indeed it could be said that Festo's story could not be told accurately without reference to Michael Cassidy and African Enterprise. These two men working together during those politically charged and emotional days constitute a unique story.

Michael Cassidy's programme is hectic. Yet he made the time not only to read my manuscript but to assist, correct, reword where necessary, and added his own remembrances and anecdotes. He has been more than generous with help. I owe him a great deal.

Beulah, my wife, who is an indefatigable servant of the gospel helped me with typing from time to time and gave me every encouragement to do this work.

Thanks to all of you.

Frank Retief
November 2012

INTRODUCTION

One of my great joys in life has been to be part of the lives of many theological students over the years. One thing I ask them to include in their reading is biographies. As a young student myself I inhabited that part of our library which harboured the section called 'Biography'. There in quiet and reflective moments I read about a large army of characters who usually had unpromising beginnings but ended up doing truly significant work for the glory of God. Evangelists, pastors, missionaries, social reformers, inner-city mission founders and a host of others passed through my mind. As I read about these exploits for God, often at the cost of great suffering, a silent longing, almost a prayer, entered my thinking, 'O God, please let me be like them.'

In later years I tried to pass on my enthusiasm for biographies to others. One of the difficulties I encountered, living in South Africa, was that all my heroes were white and western. I thus became aware that the really brilliant and exceptionally talented young African students I was talking to needed to hear of African heroes. In fact all South African Christians of whatever culture needed to know about the heroic things Africans have done in Africa. So it was that I took a new interest in Festo Kivengere, the famous Ugandan bishop.

Bishop Festo died on Wednesday 18 May 1988. This makes his death relatively recent and it means that there are many people alive today who knew him, heard him or were in some way impacted by him. Although I myself never met him, I did hear him speak at the Lausanne Conference in Switzerland in 1974. The tremendous impact of his life as a gospel evangelist cries out for his story to be retold and remembered by younger men serving in Africa today. He was always the evangelist and his contagious love for Christ, clarity of preaching and love for his hearers made him a legend in his day. Festo Kivengere is of course not the only African Christian leader whose story needs to be retold. In fact there were many others during that particular period whom God greatly used in Africa. But for now I point to several reasons why his story would have special interest for all who are concerned with the task of evangelism.

1. He was an African amongst Africans

Born in an isolated rural area in southern Uganda, he grew up as any other African boy in a culture that centred almost all of life on cattle. He lived in a kraal (simple mud and grass huts, built closely together) and tended his father's cattle by day. He listened to the stories of the village elders around the fire at night. He lived with the superstitions and taboos of most rural African people. He lived at a time when rural people had to be careful of attacks by lions and hyenas. Moreover he was of royal blood, being the grandson of a local king. His early life was not without its hardships and sadnesses but he survived it all to become the best-known evangelist in Africa in his day, travelling to many parts of the world, often in the company of Billy Graham.

2. He was the product of a revival

Through the ministry of missionaries associated with what was then called the Ruanda (later called Rwanda) Mission, a mysterious revival broke out, spread all over and, it was claimed, lasted for over fifty years. Revivals are not often spoken about today. It is almost as if many parts of the Christian church have forgotten how, over the centuries, the Holy Spirit seemed to be poured out in special power amongst Christians, impressing upon them the greatness and holiness of God, resulting in penitence and restitution, and special ability and courage in speaking to friends and neighbours about Christ and his claim to be the only Saviour of the world.

Festo became a Christian against this background. His views of what happened during these years, his own experience and his peculiar ability to move thousands when he preached invite all young preachers today to enquire into these things.

3. He was a lay evangelist for years before he was ordained

Festo was forty-seven years old when he was ordained to the Anglican priesthood in Pennsylvania after graduating from the Pittsburgh Theological Seminary. He had already been preaching for over twenty-five years as a lay evangelist with enormous effect, sustaining himself financially by his schoolteaching. This fact alone should encourage those who may never have the opportunity for a formal ordination but who nevertheless are given significant opportunities to preach the gospel. Ordination was never Bishop Festo's aim or ambition but it came along at the right time in his life when it would enable him to serve more effectively — especially when dealing with his country's leaders.

4. He took the risk of being the first prominent black man from Independent Africa to team up with a white man from South Africa

Michael Cassidy is a gifted evangelist and a visionary leader in South Africa. Cassidy had founded Africa Evangelistic Enterprise while he was studying at Fuller Seminary in the 1960s. Cassidy invited Festo to lead the AEE team in East Africa. After some hesitation he accepted. This was a huge public relations risk for Festo as South Africa was then very much an apartheid country. But by doing so he and Michael Cassidy demonstrated the unity of the gospel. They developed a style of tandem preaching — one preaching first, the other following, and finally a team for evangelism was established that modelled the unity of the body of Christ.

5. He lived through the reign of Idi Amin

Idi Amin came to power in Uganda through a military coup in January 1971. His rule was brutal. The number of people killed during his regime is reckoned to be in the hundreds of thousands. He was deposed in 1978, but during these terror-filled years Bishop Festo and other leaders in Uganda had to take a stand, often confronting Amin at risk of their lives. This kind of evangelical courage is desperately needed once again.

6. He stayed true to the gospel message until the very end

Bishop Festo finally succumbed to leukaemia in 1988 and when he did the evangelical world mourned. Festo's fame, popularity and gifts placed many stresses upon him. Not least was the constant tension between a very hectic international preaching programme and his diocesan duties back home in Uganda. But wherever he went he not only presented Christ as Saviour but seemed to radiate him. Once the new birth occurred and by grace he had moved away from shallow and superficial 'commitments' and Christian nominalism, there was no holding back. The reality of the risen and living Christ gripped him and was central to his ministry to the end.

Festo Kivengere stands as a stark reminder that personal background and disadvantages are no obstacle to a sovereign God. Moreover his story is a reminder of both the reality and the need for revival — that sovereign and gracious outpouring of the Holy Spirit that enables the Church to be the Church, and to make a lasting impact. Furthermore Festo Kivengere is a testament to the unique place the special gifts of the evangelist have in God's plan.

7. Festo Kivengere's story takes place within the framework of the Anglican Church in Uganda and is inextricably linked to the ministry of African Enterprise, launched by Michael Cassidy in the early 1960s.

Although there were many other denominations which had a role in the East African revival and although many other people often crossed his path, Festo himself was an Anglican. Later on, as he grew in spiritual experience, the Anglican boundaries would mean little, but his denominational context is helpful to remember.

1

EARLY DAYS

Festo Kivengere was born in a grim hut in a settlement called Kitazigurukwa — 'the place of the very long grass'. It was situated in the region of Rujumbura in the Kigezi district in the south-western region of Uganda. His tribe, the Bahima, had no calendars so they remembered dates by certain important events. For Kivengere's parents they remembered his birth year by a great rinderpest (cattle plague) which swept through the region and thus enabled Kivengere later to date his birth to 1919. The actual day he did not know and with good humour arbitrarily claimed 1 November (All Saints' Day) as his birthday.

The Bahima was a ruling clan from the wider tribal family of the Bahororo. Festo himself was of the royal family, grandson to the king Makobore, whose rule extended widely throughout Rujumbura.

During childhood he would hear many stories around the kraal fires, about the history of his people, their battles for land and cattle and slaves of famous family members. His people were pastoralists who herded their cattle as did generations before them. The whole of life centred on their cattle. Cattle were the centre of everything and each cow was named. His grandfather Makobore was both king and priest of his tribe. He was a huge man, famed as a warrior in his youth and a fair ruler. Makobore signed a treaty with the British in 1912, acknowledging British rule, which was mediated through a Baganda advisor. He also welcomed the first Church Missionary Society missionary about that time, who founded a small church. He eventually handed his rule over to his son Karegyesa. Kivengere grew up with a sense of superiority which he later saw as unfortunate and superficial. This superiority was greatly modified by his conversion to Christianity, but nevertheless he had installed in him a sense of confidence which was a huge help in later life when he became a much loved evangelist and church leader.

Kivengere's mother was called Barungi which means 'beautiful'. She became something of a legend when Kivengere was growing up because of her strong-willed personality, individualism and personal enterprise. She had been married before to a wealthy cattle owner, but a man who was a drunk and a wife beater. Her father exercised his kingly prerogative to dissolve the marriage. She had to leave her baby son behind but she was free of a brutal marriage.

She then married Ntzisira, also a wealthy cattle owner, but an older and kinder man. He had been widowed and had four daughters who were brought up by relatives. He was Kivengere's father and he chose the name 'Kivengere' for his son, after a close friend. It was an unusual name but his mother soon had a nickname for her little boy, 'Akasikina', which means 'Little Hiccup', and by which he was known throughout his childhood.

Kivengere's father was a gentle-natured man who never raised his hand or his voice to anyone. The young Kivengere at least at this time of his life experienced the warmth of a happy family.

Because of the importance of cattle, about six years after his birth Kivengere's father decided to move the family to a tiny village called Kyamakanda where the grass was richer and the country was ideal for cattle. It was a wilder area where there were often problems with lion and hyena.

The next few years were happy ones for Kivengere. Although the British rule had brought in a new form of law and order, the colonial presence hardly touched his life in Rujumbura district. The result was that Kivengere was brought up in a very traditional Bahima culture, and with the responsibilities of a cattle herder. Although his childhood days were carefree there was routine of some kind, all centring on the needs of the cattle — watering, watching, milking, herding and counting. Kivengere's early diet was almost solely the traditional diet of milk and boiled cattle blood whipped up with salt and butter, sometimes with banana or potatoes. The average Bahima child only began to eat solids seriously at about the age of fourteen.

Every night as a child for Kivengere was highlighted by stories around the fire. In addition to the tales of their ancestors, they talked incessantly about their cattle. Many of the stories were dramatically told with performances and stick twirling and long rapid recitations. Young children memorized songs and lists of cattle names, and the men told stories about their hunting. It was natural to Kivengere to think on his feet and to speak fluently and to improvise, and thus it is easy to see how God was preparing this young boy for his greater work in later life. Kivengere had a young friend Bugaari. The two were inseparable and together they learned the laws, taboos and beliefs of the Bahima people. The Bahima believed in God as a great creator spirit whom they called Ruhanga, which Kivengere explained as follows.

> Long before the missionaries came to Africa my people knew there was a God. And we wanted Him, we desired Him. We knew He was the Creator, and so we tried to worship Him. We sacrificed to Him and we believed our security came from Him. Our problem was never, is there a God, but how can we reach Him?

They resorted to the world of spirits and the occult. They believed in ancestral spirits who were, on the whole, benign. Sacrifices of milk or meat would be made to them. Then there were the Bachwezi or the 'bigger spirits' who it was believed could stir or visit whole villages. Witchdoctors were needed to deal with these frightening malevolent spirits. Kivengere had memories of a time when wave upon wave of 'big spirits' came to Kyamakanda.

> People were thrown into frenzies of hysterical chanting, speaking in unknown tongues and times of unrestrained worship around the fire
>
> (*Authorized Biography of Festo Kivengere*, p. 39).

Festo and his friends went through the normal initiation rites common to all the young boys and were warned to keep the secrets of the tribe. The whole ceremony was taken very seriously. However, important as all these features of Bahima life were to the young Kivengere, other events were beginning to unfold which would have a lasting impact on him.

The first of these events was the arrival of Constance Hornsby to Kivengere's village. Constance Hornsby was a middle-aged English woman who was a missionary midwife with the Rwanda Mission. She went throughout the villages of Kigezi, the general district where Kivengere lived with his family, recruiting women and girls for reading classes in the town of Kabale. The idea of a school was a very new idea for the people and it took a lot of courage for her to come as she did with her proposal. Her arrival in Kyamakanda is so hilariously described in Kivengere's official biography by Anne Coomes it is worth quoting.

> 'Our parents told us children that morning that we had to be very, very careful that day. A pink lady was on her way to the village, coming along the paths like one of us! My mother warned me, "These pink people are dangerous ... there have been stories of people disappearing and that they eat people."' Barungi and the other women were all staying indoors, just in case.
>
> Kivengere and Bugaari were jittery and immensely excited. They led their calves to the top of a small hillock, from where they could command a good view of the path from the nearest village, Kebisoni. Bugaari recalls the exact moment the two boys saw their first white person:

'Suddenly, over the brow of the hill came the strangest person. Her face and arms were pink — for a minute we doubted she had any skin. She had the strangest looking head.' (She was wearing a pith helmet.) Some Bahima men were carrying her along in a sling chair of bamboo. Others followed along behind, carrying all her luggage

(p. 14).

Although his grandfather had met white people and had negotiated with them, this was Kivengere's first experience with whites. But Constance Hornsby made friends that day. She was well received and the young Kivengere had his first brush with Christianity.

A second major change for Kivengere occurred a few months after Miss Hornsby's visit. His father, Ntzisira, contracted tuberculosis and died.

His father's death meant that his mother Barungi and her children had to leave the hut. She also had to marry again and chose her husband's nephew Rwabugarame as her husband. Kivengere was sent to live with his grandfather Makobore for a while. He was ten years old; his happy childhood was nearing its end.

At his grandfather's kraal, where his Uncle Karegyesa ruled as chief, Kivengere was introduced to many visitors and various comings and goings. But a third event occurred. A catechist arrived in Rukungiri and built a little mud church nearby. His grandfather and his uncle had been baptized as Christians and had enormous respect for the Christian faith in spite of very little knowledge of it. His grandfather took him to a church service which left him mystified. The catechist was encouraged while the family simply carried on with their spirit worship. It seemed very small and unpromising but Christianity had arrived and big events would occur later.

Kivengere returned to live with his mother and her new husband. The marriage was not a happy one but the new husband was at least tolerant of his new wife's offspring. However, possibly the biggest of all changes to Kivengere's young life was about to occur.

One day a man named Byensi arrived in the village. He was known to the people as someone who had been born there. He had disappeared sometime before, but now he returned as a Christian, and constructed a church. He had been trained to read and write and he was willing to share his knowledge with all who would care to listen. He was there with the king's permission and soon had a clan of young boys to instruct, who had been released from herding. Without this small, very humble beginning, and learning to read, Kivengere would probably have remained a cattle herder all his life. Following a CMS tradition that went back to 1877 converts had been given the title 'reader' simply because they were usually the only literate people in their areas.

It turned out that Kivengere was a very good pupil. He learned his letters by drawing them in the sand with a sharp stick and soon he was instructing others in learning their letters. In May 1930 he earned a certificate that said he could read. He was presented with a Gospel and became an official 'reader'. The Gospel of Luke became his companion. He read it regularly and as the little church school progressed so his own traditional beliefs seemed to fade and he made a childlike profession of faith in Jesus Christ.

Byensi, the reader and teacher, instructed the boys carefully in the basics of Christianity. He taught them strict morals. The teaching was not perfect and probably tended to be legalistic but it was the best he knew.

Perhaps a lesson we all need to relearn in Christian leadership and mission is that not all truth is grasped at once. Truth often needs time to percolate in our hearts and minds. Therefore we should never despise small beginnings in the life of anybody learning the Christian faith.

Byensi chose Kivengere to be his assistant in the collecting of supplies for the little mission church, which entailed a fifty-mile journey. For a boy who had never left his home territory it was a big adventure and a harbinger of the thousands of miles he would one day travel in his work as an evangelist.

He was baptized in November 1930 with sixty other candidates. He was given the name of Festo because his godparents wanted a name from the Bible. In their naive state they viewed all Bible names as holy so Festus from Acts 26:24 was adapted by adding an 'O'.

It was a great event for young Festo. He expressed his excitement as follows:

My thoughts that night were very serious indeed. I thoroughly expected that from now on I would put all sin behind me and lead a good, pure, godly life. I would read the Bible, obey all the laws, and live up to the very highest of ethical standards. I wanted God, I desired God. I didn't yet realise that God never expected me to 'be a really good person' under my own steam.

But Festo felt disappointed after the event. He had no overwhelming experience. He thought great spiritual power would descend on him and that holiness would be quite natural. Instead the old struggles to 'be good' were still there. Nevertheless his commitment was as real as his eleven-year-old understanding could permit. The next step was that he was enrolled in a new little school on Kinyasano Hill at Rukungiri, six miles from home.

The school was run by missionaries who were in touch with the Rwanda missionaries. It was a simple bush school of mud and branches but it was an introduction to formal education. From our vantage point it is hard to imagine the excitement of learning to those who have never had the privilege. Festo had to care for the calves before he could begin the six-mile journey to school. And his path to school took him through lion, leopard and snake-infested country. Coming home at night was hazardous and there were stories of students killed in those days.

Festo thrived. He was naturally healthy and strong, and was supported and encouraged by his family. He was serious about his studies and impatient with those who wasted time. But like all young boys he loved the barefoot football games they played when classes ended. A dip in the river followed the football, then the long walk home.

However, his home was becoming increasingly unhappy. His stepfather regularly beat his mother and Festo grew up hating him. His mother's distress drew the mother and son close together. Her strong character and refusal to indulge in bitterness deeply affected him. To Festo she was the ideal woman and had enormous influence on the wife he would choose, the way he brought up his daughters, and the opportunities he would one day create for women to serve in his diocese.

Festo eventually moved to his uncle's home. He was the county chief and a man of great influence. He was a huge man with a great presence. He had recently married a woman who had become a Christian. He wholeheartedly supported the little school near his home and wanted his young nephew to benefit by living closer to the school. His uncle's kraal was now a government headquarters and Festo benefited from all he saw and heard. His mother moved with him to his new home. Festo did extremely well at school and finally graduated to Kigezi High School. His friend Bugaari joined him and they went to a school run by British missionaries, with all the changes that meant in terms of strict discipline and time-keeping. He was introduced to potatoes and beans but missed the warm blood and smoked milk. He was sixteen years old.

Festo flourished at school. His nature was cheerful and friendly, and he was well liked by all. He joined the Boys Brigade, playing drums, and he matured under the leadership of the Rev. Lawrence Barham. His worlds were merging. He moved increasingly from fear and superstition into education, liberation and Christianity.

When Festo returned to school for the autumn term in 1935 he discovered that Lawrence Barham was organizing a convention in Kabale. The speakers at this convention were a team of people from Gahini, and a team of Africans were coming, led by Dr Joe Church.

This is a good point to pause and reflect on the backdrop of revival that colours the story of Festo Kivengere. The outpouring of the Spirit was already occurring in several places and was soon to sweep up the young Kivengere in its mighty power.

2

A God-sized vision

Some people believe that the presence of evil in the world and the existence of pain is an indication that God does not exist. One would think that in the face of the wars and sufferings the world endures, the level of faith in God may drop and finally disappear altogether. However, while it is true that such a response may occur from time to time, the stark fact of the matter is that even though often unheralded, unreported or underreported, the work of God in building his kingdom keeps going on, sometimes with amazing momentum.

There have been sporadic reports of what could be called 'spiritual revival' especially in Africa, since 1860 and probably long before that. During these special times of spiritual refreshing the most amazing things happen. For instance the 'revival' scholar Dr Edwin Orr reported in his *Evangelical Awakenings in Africa* that during the Anglo Boer War soldiers on both sides of the divide came into contact with the desperate needs of the indigenous people of South Africa. 'In 1903 a hundred evangelical British soldiers were

reported returning to South Africa to serve the common
Lord of Boer and Briton in reaching the Bantu folk with
the Good News' (p. 135). Also little known is the fact that
after centuries of hostilities the Boer general, General
Beyers, called for a meeting in Warmbad on 3 October. 'One
hundred demobilized men contacted the Cape Missionary
Committee and were assigned to the care of Bethel, a
mission station near Pietersburg' (p. 135).

All of this was part of the outworking of the great move of
God's Spirit which took place amongst the Dutch Reformed
Church in 1860 and amongst the Methodists in 1866. Not
only so, but similar wonderful works of God took place
in several countries in Africa. These included, in what
was known then as South West Africa, works among the
Hereros; in Malawi among the Ngoni; and Congo, Angola,
Cameroon, Tanganyika, Mombasa and then in 1905 Uganda,
Nigeria, Ghana and the Ivory Coast (as then known) also
experienced a vast stirring up of revival.

It should be noted that these manifested themselves
amongst the crowds as public prayer and confessing of sins,
sometimes uncontrollable crying and a great awareness of
spiritual realities. But there were usually huge responses to
the evangelical message and an intense evangelistic fervour
followed (p. 139). For instance, in Zambia, Don Crawford, a
British missionary, met a man carrying a string with more
than thirty knots, each representing a convert won for Christ.
In addition, 'feuds were healed, debts paid, bitter quarrelling
gave way to brotherly kindness, prayer became joyous,
candidates volunteered for Christian service, and heathens
brought into the Christian faith' (p. 139).

In 1925 the first Anglican missionaries entered the twin kingdoms of Rwanda – Burundi and gained a foothold at Gahini where an effective medical and evangelistic ministry was begun. The Rwanda General and Medical Mission was an evangelical Anglican society which was an arm of the Church Missionary Society.

It was sponsored largely by those Anglican churches that had been influenced by the strong biblical evangelical and Protestant emphasis embodied by the Keswick Convention in England. This stressed the vital importance of an individual relationship with God characterized by personal holiness, turning from evil, confessing sins and striving consistently for the 'higher life' by being filled with the Spirit. Its pioneers included Dr A. C. Stanley Smith, son of Stanley Smith who was one of the famous Cambridge seven who served in China (p. 159).

Amongst many of the key personalities, both African and European, who were in Rwanda when it experienced an outpouring of the Spirit was Dr Joe Church. Dr Church was a medical missionary supported by the Cambridge Inter — Collegiate Christian Union (CICCU). He left behind what could have been a prestigious career back home to become a medical missionary. Educated in the best English schools and cultivated in 'proper' English ways, he arrived in Gahini in Rwanda in 1928. Within his first year he was overwhelmed by the region's needs. Hansen and Woodbridge write as follows:

> 250,000 Africans living around Gahini had no prior access to medicine or the Gospel. His hospital was a collection of huts

fashioned from grass. He and other missionaries used them
to distribute food to the famine-starved masses. Some days,
1,000 refugees fleeing famine passed through Gahini.

'The shacks were packed with thin apathetic people sitting
over the embers of their fires, just waiting, many of them
lying about ill with fever and exhaustion and covered with
the disease of yaws and flies,' Church remembered. 'They
held their hands out begging as we passed and some of the
naked children tried to run after us a little way.'

What Church witnessed day after day would be enough to
bring the strongest man to tears. Just before going to sleep
one night, Church and fellow missionary Bert Jackson heard
what they thought to be a jackal in the garden. 'With a
torch and shotgun we searched,' Church wrote. 'The strange
noise went on from time to time and then stopped, so after
finding nothing we went to bed. The next morning I found
a completely naked starving man who had crawled as far
as the garden and died.' Around this same time, Jackson
asked Church to help him check on a stench emanating
from something in his bathtub. 'We pulled aside a sheet and
found a living skeleton of a boy, just alive, who had crawled
into the bathroom and pulled a sheet over him and gone to
sleep,' Church said. 'He was covered from head to foot in
sores.'

Church was discouraged and angered by the apathetic
attitude of fellow workers at his primitive hospital. But
a year later he travelled to Namirembe Hill in Kampala,
Uganda. At the Anglican cathedral Joe Church met and
made a new friend named Simeon Nsibambi. A successful

and sophisticated professional man, Nsibambi was Uganda's chief health officer. He had been longing for a more powerful and intimate experience with God. He and Joe Church discussed the Keswick teaching on the filling of the Spirit. He, Church, and a friend he had brought with him studied the Scofield Bible together and ended up praying, renouncing sin and 'claiming the victorious life'. The three of them also prayed for revival for the Uganda church.

The reader needs to bear in mind the era in which these men lived. Medically, few of the medicines used today were available, not too much technology was available for the missionaries and the Uganda church was only about fifty years old. Yet, notwithstanding its relative newness as a church, amazingly by 1893 Uganda had already commissioned 260 evangelists. The entire Bible had been translated and widely distributed, and churches welcomed others from across tribal barriers. But by the time Joe Church arrived the church had largely sunk into nominalism.

This small prayer meeting between Joe Church, Simeon Nsibambi and a friend had a profound impact. Simeon found himself spontaneously witnessing to others. He abandoned his western name and dress and adopted a robe, sold his belongings and became a preacher with great success around Kampala.

An invigorated Joe Church returned to Rwanda. A new concern for eternal matters, mainly amongst workers and other missions, became demonstrable. Early morning prayer meetings were established as revival took hold of the area. The revival was accompanied by conviction and confession of sin under great emotional stress. Congregations spent 'whole nights in prayer, followed by great joy and zeal to win others'. Evangelical teams developed and entire regions experienced revival. Conventions were set up where the movement was able to sustain its focus on holiness, reconciliation and evangelism. The churches who were revived became known as 'those on fire' or 'those who glow'.

Influenced by Keswick theology they managed to avoid the fixation with signs and wonders. Rather, the main distinctives of this revival were repentance, reconciliation, holiness, prayer, evangelism and kindness to all. This is not to deny that this revival did not cause problems. There were many instances of emotional excess, false conversions, rifts between different groups and a drift amongst some to a form of legalism on the matters of confession and repentance. There were also occasions when a lack of wisdom or sensitivity caused unnecessary difficulties. But all in all this revival had a massive impact on church life in East Africa. It is said that it lasted for fifty years, making it the longest continuous revival in history (p. 165).

To understand the power and influence of Festo Kivengere it is important to keep this East African revival largely in mind. It did not begin with Kivengere but it forms the backdrop to his life and ministry. His own emergence as a Christian leader took place against this background and formed the context of the development of his own views and preaching style.

3

EARLY RELIGIOUS

EXPERIENCE

Dr Joe Church and his friends in Gahini were constantly seeking for a further blessing of the Holy Spirit. After the first ten years the Rwanda Mission had much for which to praise God. There had been 5,000 public baptisms, and 300 village churches had been established. Two general hospitals, boys' and girl's schools, and twenty-nine missionaries divided between two mission stations — Gahini and Kabale, where Festo was at school.

Joe Church reported that in all areas Christians were becoming more discontented with the state of the church and were developing a new realization of the meaning and the power of prayer. By April 1931 there were early morning prayer meetings at Joe Church's home. Soon a pattern developed — a week-long teaching convention followed by confirmation services led by Bishop Stuart of Uganda. Crowds began to attend the church services.

Joe Church developed the idea of 'brokenness which made it possible for God to pour out His Holy Spirit'. Whatever many may think of this approach today this particular emphasis served to help many to understand repentance. 'Brokenness' became a byword of the revival.

At the end of 1933, a simple event occurred which had wide ramifications. Two white missionaries apologized to their African brothers for wrong attitudes. None of the Africans had ever heard a white person admit that they were wrong. Their amazement was accompanied by a new sense of unity.

Then on 27 December of the same year a conference of African evangelists, teachers and missionaries was disrupted when formal prayers broke down. A sense of conviction swept over the whole assembly. Prayer became intense and was accompanied by confession of sin and much weeping. This in turn was followed by forgiveness of each other and thanksgiving. People were possessed by a strong sense of love for others, for Christ and an overwhelming joy. The missionaries saw that as soon as they had repented of prejudice and superiority, new relationships developed and the character of their work was altered.

Early 1934 saw great excitement at Gahini. The members of this new movement were called Abaruwaka — 'those on fire'. But the intensity of what was being expressed also carried some backlash with dissensions and divisions. Thus much time was given at the prayer meetings for people to 'put things right' with each other. Then a large team went out on an evangelistic mission. This was to be followed in 1935 with a visit to Kabale where Festo was at school. Thus when he and his friends arrived for the new school term in 1935 he watched curiously as the team of thirteen led by Joe Church arrived from Gahini.

Festo was not particularly moved by the convention. The preaching was saying nothing he had not heard before, although he acknowledged that there was a difference in how they said it. He sensed a power in them and was riveted by their shining faces and obvious love for God.

Joe Church read from the Scofield Bible and each day preached on a different subject: sin, repentance, new birth, 'coming out of Egypt', and the victorious Christian life. A praise meeting concluded the convention and people went home. Nothing spectacular had happened but people were subdued and startled by what they heard.

But soon strange stories began to do the rounds. People began to weep unexpectedly, dream dreams of heaven or cry out under conviction. A sense of sin came upon many. Some gatherings were impacted by people trembling and weeping for their sins. Then there was a breakthrough when a person felt forgiven and saved by Christ. This was followed by overwhelming love and joy. At that time Festo was deeply struck by the well-known illustration of a boy who made a boat, lost it, saw it for sale in a shop and bought it back, concluding with the words, 'Now you are mine twice over.'

This story made him yearn for a relationship with God that he knew he did not possess, in spite of his childhood commitment. He was further amazed one day to discover that his good friend Bugaari had joined the 'burning ones'. He had been born again.

Festo discovered that about 5.00am each morning students arose to attend an early prayer meeting before they cultivated the school fields where they grew their own food. Furthermore they were meeting for prayer in a little storeroom. Barham in turn reported that after the Kabale Convention the whole surrounding district had been impacted by people confessing sin, restitution being made, sins abandoned and evangelistic teams going throughout the district. This was the time the laity took the task of evangelism out of the hands of the clergy and did it themselves.

A new missionary arrived in the person of the Reverend Philip (Pip) Tribe. He was a committed evangelical with a Keswick Convention background, but like Festo did not know what to make of all the repenting, weeping and talk of brokenness. However he impressed Festo and had a great influence on him because he was the first white man to invite Festo into his home.

In January the following year (1936) Festo was invited to join the storeroom prayer group. He went along gladly so that he could ask questions about being born again. Then early one morning Festo came to a point of what he thought was surrender to Christ. It seemed real enough at the time but subsequent experiences in his life suggested that this initial response to the gospel lacked depth and reality. However, at this point in his spiritual journey, it all felt real to him. He remembers:

There was no weeping, no hysteria — the dormitory beyond the flimsy door was full of sleeping boys. But I knew immediately something had changed within me. What I had read about Jesus in the Gospels came alive in a way it had not done before. I had suddenly caught the vision of the gracious God, the Creator, who had come in Jesus Christ to seek me
(Anne Coomes' *Biography*, p. 72).

Soon he was confessing his sins and faults and had joined the weekend evangelism teams. Such teams became a hallmark of the revival. Festo had a talent for public speaking and as he went around with his friends he found signs of the revival all around. Conversions led to people paying their debts, paying their taxes and returning their stolen cattle.

His family's response to his conversion was cautious. His mother was not sure that such a vision as they had of Christ was suitable for a woman of her aristocratic clan. His uncle was puzzled by the disposing of long-held tribal customs.

But with thousands being converted from 1935 onwards the revival was to make a shattering impact. For the pagans were never left alone... By 1941 there would be few homes in North Kigezi, which covered hundreds of square miles, where a family, however isolated, could honestly say they had never heard of Jesus

(*Biog.*, p. 74).

But as is often the case when God works in unusual ways, not everybody was impressed. There were divisions and anger within the Ugandan church. Not everybody appreciated the face-to-face challenges, the hysterical weeping, the all-night prayer and singing meetings and for that matter the closer black/white relationships. The catchword of the revival was AWAKE. Questions were put to the church. Why do we tolerate nominalism? Why allow people who are living in open sin to the Lord's Table?

The proponents of the revival were also at times divisive with their excessive displays of emotions and hysteria which to some extent was probably culturally conditioned. But then it needs to be remembered that there were many new converts from totally pagan backgrounds.

The revival caused a crisis for the Anglican Church in Uganda. It had the potential to tear itself away from the Church and set up a new rival church. But God had given the Church a gift in Bishop Stuart who was gracious and forebearing and was able to deal wisely with the situation.

Festo eventually went to Mbarara High School. His advance to high school was overshadowed by the shock of hearing that his mother, left on her own at home, faced a lioness by herself. The animal was after one of the herd and she beat it off with a stick. His admiration for his mother knew no bounds.

Festo now began to think about his long-term future and wanted to become a teacher.

4

RELAPSE AND
RESTORATION

Festo turned his back on Christianity soon after his arrival at high school. The reason for this was curious. He had felt the impulse during the holidays to tell the people in his uncle's household about his faith and to 'put right' certain things with them. He did not do so and thus lived with the feeling that in some way he had betrayed his Lord. Thus he displayed the dangers that lurk for Christians when they succumb to subjective urges that are based on a commonly accepted set of beliefs which are not necessarily supported by Scripture.

The years that followed became increasingly dark for him. He had lost the inner sense of peace he had enjoyed and instead despair set in. He became hardened and sought distraction from various Christian influences that surrounded him at school. He fell in with a group of lads untouched by the revival or Christian witness around them. He joined them in their escapades to the shops after dark and began to drink and smoke heavily. This only increased his sense of guilt and more and more he distanced himself from the Christians around him. When term broke for holidays Festo and Bugaari walked the seventy-five miles back to his home at Rukungiri. While at home his mother told him she was going to leave her husband. According to Bahima custom Festo would soon be old enough to take responsibility for her and for his father's herd of cattle which he would inherit.

His mother requested more information about this Jesus the Christians worshipped, but the son she spoke to now was very different from the son who had gone to school. She was now more interested than he was and he was unable to help her. Thus she remained a pagan but was very 'warm towards Jesus' (p. 79).

Although his inner misery continued, Festo was serious about his education and planned to attend King's College at Budo, then obtain a diploma at Makerere College. Teachers were in great demand and Festo's personality was very suited to this task. In the end he attended Bishop Tucker College at Mukono.

Before he left college he took his mother away from her husband who had beaten her savagely. He took her back to the village where his real father had been born.

At college Festo gave himself to his studies but continued to run with the wilder students on drinking sprees. Although surrounded by reminders of his former spiritual commitment Festo maintained a nominal relationship with the church and continued to carry his increasing guilt.

It is worth pausing for a moment to ask how such a state of affairs could arise after his experience with revival and his former professed conversion experience. Special times of grace have occurred many times in history and experiences like that of Festo's have often been displayed during such times. One needs to remember that the path of spiritual conversion to Christ and development afterwards is not always successful and trouble free. Nor does it always follow the neat agenda we map out for these experiences, in our minds.

Apart from the natural tendency of the fallen human heart to be spiritually deceived either by wrong teaching or by putting too much emphasis on subjective experiences, there is always the sinister presence of the devil. As the enemy of God he seeks constantly to destroy God's work in human hearts. Often even among sincere Christians, times will come when a veil seems to drop over the heart and a period of intense spiritual struggle ensues. We also need to remember that conversion to Christ is not always immediate and clear cut. Often there are apparent conversions which are not conversions at all, but rather steps along the way. True conversion can happen in stages and may sometimes be accompanied by great inner spiritual struggles. It is also wise to remember that sometimes there are false conversions, where no spiritual life is imparted but only a superficial interest in the message of the gospel. Whatever the true state of Festo's spiritual condition at this time in his life, we can nevertheless see the powerful impact of a very sensitive but perhaps wrongly informed conscience in his life. So Festo entered into his college and training years in a deep spiritual vacuum.

Nevertheless he made considerable progress with his studies. He also discovered an uncanny ability to communicate with students of all ages. He had a natural tendency to leadership and a calm authoritative presence.

In 1938 his mother died. She was only about fifty years of age but had borne years of brutal beatings and hard toil. After the funeral he had to make arrangements for his three younger siblings and over 100 cows which were now his responsibility. He was nineteen. He found a relative who would bring up the children, and the milk from the cows would pay expenses. Festo missed his mother and mourned deeply for her. Nevertheless he knew he had to face the future realistically.

The Second World War began in 1939 and those who had radios tuned in. For Festo and his friends, stories of mass bombing, tanks and machine guns were beyond their imagination. But the outbreak of war meant teachers became very thin on the ground. Kigezi High School wrote to the college pleading for the early release of teachers to help them or they would have to close their classes.

Festo, still feeling his bereavement, was glad to be chosen to leave early to help the school. It meant he would be near his remaining family to care for them. Young men from all over Uganda were joining the British forces but Festo was sent back to the very school from which he started. He was delighted. All he wanted to do was teach.

While Festo was grappling with his emotions and war was spreading across Europe, the revival continued in Uganda.

But many tensions continued to surface even amongst the missionaries because the more hysterical weeping and praying meant many services had to be abandoned.

The revival spread to the Sudan and to Tanganyika. There were reports of thousands of conversions and many spiritual blessings, accompanied by other reports of many unbalanced excesses. Even the missionary evangelistic team going from church to church came under scrutiny by the government. The war made everybody suspicious and the revival did not help because many of the meetings left in their wake hysterical conversions which disrupted village life and led to tension between the traditional Africans and the new Christians. The revival became a mixed blessing.

When Festo returned home to Rujumbura he got a shock. As he passed through the market place he saw some people gathered singing hymns in public. Then as he arrived home his favourite niece Kyabyarwa met him, threw her arms around him and said, 'Uncle Festo, welcome home! I love Jesus now. Do you too?' The biggest part of his spiritual battle was about to begin. Festo felt that 'God's finger followed me and my conscience was ill at ease. When you know the truth and rebel against it, you become strangely hard' (*Biog.*, p. 89). By now Festo had become a drunkard (p. 90).

The school provided him with a home and he moved in, with his stepsister Eva and his niece Kyabyarwa in one bedroom, his nine-year-old stepbrother Jonathan in another, and himself into the third. He had hoped to have a happy family but the relationship with his sister and niece were strained because they had joined the revival. They kept on telling

him that he needed Jesus and that without Jesus he was
going to hell. His resentment turned into anger and when he
had been drinking heavily his homecomings could be very
unpleasant and the girls became afraid of him.

The ensuing days were difficult for Festo. The intensity of
the revival in the town was increasing. It had begun in an
ordinary Anglican service one Sunday during the Bible
reading. The congregation started to weep and the Bible
reading broke down. People claimed to have found Christ in
a new and personal way. Soon the congregation could not fit
into the church and so spread out in small groups meeting
under trees, or in homes all through North Kigezi. People
would talk about Jesus everywhere and it was not unknown
for the night to burst into song. Many of his former friends
had groups of people meeting in their homes and singing.
People would call out to him so that it was hard to slip away
unnoticed.

Festo found an ally in his Uncle Karegyesa, and they shared
their resentment of the revival with each other. Many of the
traditional taboos were ignored and distinctions between
tribal clans were increasingly not observed. Karegyesa
arranged for some of the Christians to be beaten up and
indeed some were. But he called off the beatings when the
beaters explained that they couldn't sleep at night. In the
morning some of them ran off weeping to join the very
people they had beaten up.

Because Festo was teaching in a mission school he had to
attend church services. Almost all the services were led by
the 'fanatics' and all sermons led to Jesus. He was finding

life increasingly unmanageable and confusing, but still he stubbornly dug in his heels.

In spite of his differences with those around him his personal popularity soared. He always dressed smartly which made a great impression on the boys. Festo tells the story of the embarrassing day when it was his turn to take the morning chapel service.

> I didn't like it at all. I knew, and the boys knew, that I had nothing to give. It was embarrassing, but somehow I managed to admit, 'Boys, I have nothing to say. Has anyone of you something to tell us?' Who should stand up but my own brother! Nine years old, he came forward with his New Testament and for the next twenty-five minutes you could have heard a pin drop. He finished without calling them to make any outward sign of repentance, but about twenty boys gave their lives to the Lord. I should have got up and gone forward, but I was too proud.

In this way his school life became a strange muddle. Although he had to teach Scripture he undermined it with snide comments. His great influence on children made them love him. His bad example with drinking was known to them, but only added an extra edge for them to admire, as it always does with rebels in all societies. Other teachers and God-fearing parents were greatly disappointed in him but could not fault his teaching skills or performance. Adding to Festo's state of mind was a growing reaction to what he perceived as bossiness and paternalism on the part of some of the white missionaries — especially Gregory Smith, the district's school supervisor. Throughout 1941 and 1942 the revival Christians irritated Festo. They never missed an opportunity to plead with him to repent, often with tears in their eyes. Festo sought comfort in heavier drinking.

Even his friend Bugaari was involved and Festo ordered him out of his home. Festo found comfort with another friend also named Festo. Festo Rwamunahe had a sister whom Festo would one day marry. The two Festos considered each other as the only true teachers at the school who did not 'have a testimony'.

In March 1941 the headmaster was considering turning Festo out of the school because he had become such a drunkard (p. 96). A new young missionary named Lilian Clarke arrived to take over the Kabale girls' boarding school. She wanted to disapprove of Festo but found him clever and full of life.

The two Festos became increasingly frustrated with the revival Christians. Week after week different people wept over their sins. The market was full of people testifying. Even the British government officers in Kabale were rattled by the long queues of people forming outside their office wanting to return or pay for things. The district commander said it was hard to get any work done.

But as the days went by, he discovered that his antics with the other Festo and the young men he chose as friends no longer served as a distraction. Festo often caught his niece and sister weeping for him in their prayers.

Early October 1941 arrived. Festo had even thought of suicide. Yet for all this the job of headmaster was becoming vacant and some people tipped him for the post. On Sunday morning 4 October Festo's fourteen-year-old niece, very

bravely considering past experiences, told Festo that God
had told her and twelve-year-old Eva that their prayers for
his soul would be answered that very weekend. The next
morning it was Festo's turn to take the boys to church.
Feeling uncomfortable he sat at the back. It was an ordinary
Anglican prayer book service, but long before the preacher
stood up people were standing all over the place, repenting of
their sins and accepting the Lord. Then to his consternation
his niece leapt to her feet.

> *I want to praise God. The devil has been making me afraid
> of telling you what the Lord has done for my cousin Eva and
> me. On Friday night the Lord assured us that our prayers
> for Festo are answered. Festo is sitting in the corner right
> there, and we know that he is going to come back to the
> Lord today.*

Festo left the church furious and went to his Uncle Karegyesa's
kraal, where the two of them spent the day drinking and
mocking the revival. Late that afternoon he was wobbling
home on his bicycle when he met another cyclist. It was his
friend Festo Rwamunahe pedalling towards him. He skidded
to a halt and breathlessly told Festo Kivengere, 'Festo! Three
hours ago Jesus became a living reality to me. I know my sins
are forgiven!' (p. 99).

He then asked Festo's forgiveness for three specific matters
and promised that he would never live again the life they
had been enjoying together. He challenged Festo with the
words, 'Where are you?' and left him. Festo got home under
tremendous conviction, his hands shaking too much to light
his pipe. He then felt a strong inner compulsion to pray.

Although he did not know what to say he began to cry out to God. He said, 'God, if you happen to be there as my friends say You are, here is my life. Thoroughly empty, very much in trouble, and full of guilt, because of the wrong things I have done. Do for me what You have done for my friend Festo.'

The response to this prayer is best told in Festo's own words:

> Suddenly, as if in a vision, in front of me was Jesus hanging on the cross, as clear as anything I had ever seen with my physical eyes.

Festo later described it as Calvary 'almost as it were up before me on a screen'. He was shattered. 'For a time it seemed as if there was no one in the world except that Man hanging on the cross.' As Festo looked at him,

> I did not see just a helpless human being hanging on the cross like a criminal; I saw my God slaughtered for my sin.

This first impact made him reel. It was a realization that the death of Christ 'was because of me'.

> It was shattering, because it was as if he was saying, 'This is how bad you are.' This realization engulfed me.

But then came the second impact.

> It was as if the Lord said, 'Now that is also how much I love you.' This was almost overwhelming. To have the One I had done that to turn around and say, 'That is how much I love you,' was too much. I heard His voice. 'While you were

careless I still loved you.' His eyes of infinite love were looking into mine. I shook my head. Literally, I shook my head. 'Lord,' I whispered, 'You can't love me; I don't deserve it. I am your enemy. I am rebellious. I have been hating your people. How can You love me like that? I am opposite to these Christians; in fact I hate You, Lord.' (Notice by now I was calling him Lord — restoration had come without my knowing it!)

Christ said, 'I love you this much.' And that, of course, completely melted my heart. I began to confess my sins and to seek forgiveness, only to find that forgiveness had already taken place. I was forgiven. Guilt was no longer there.

He would later realize that there is no qualification for the love of God other than that you are a sinner, completely finished. God in love takes the initiative to meet the sinner wherever they may be.

A whole new world had opened before me. Love ran through me and filled me with such a sense of freedom and joy and I wondered what to do.

I got up off my knees, still crying but now with joy. No more guilt, no more shame. God was no longer a threat. Christ was no longer an embarrassment. He loved me! I started singing and shouting. I sang all the little songs I'd thought I'd forgotten like 'Jesus loves me this I know'. They had now, for me, a new meaning! I just wanted to praise and praise.

Suddenly Festo felt almost frightened.

'Lord,' I prayed, 'this is too much, I don't think I can live long like this. But give me permission to live for one week and I'll

*tell everybody about it. Uncles, aunts, friends.' I made plans
on the spot to tell the whole area in my last week on earth. I
was still expected in class on the following morning, so how
I thought I was going to teach and evangelise all of North
Kigezi, I can't imagine.*

He wasted no time. Immediately he went back to the church
where the service he had left some hours previously was still
continuing in the Uganda Revival style where time meant
nothing. As he came in the back of the church door, his
niece and his sister saw him and immediately realized that
something dramatic had happened and that the Lord had
heard their prayers and fulfilled their prophetic word that
Festo would come to the Lord that day. Immediately there
was a great uproar of rejoicing in the church. The young girls
and many others in the congregation raced down to the back
of the church, embraced him and rejoiced with him as the
congregation sang the Revival song 'Tuku tendereza...'

His friend Bugaari suddenly realized, 'Festo's saved!' People
hugged and danced around with him. Some beat big drums.
He had no chance to say any form of confession. Many
were clapping, dancing, singing and shrieking with joy.
They accompanied him home but his little house could not
accommodate them all, and the overflow gathered outside
his door. The celebration went on for hours while Festo,
exhausted, finally went to bed. But others stayed up all night
as a demonstration of their love for their new brother.

Although he did not know it then, the man who would
become Africa's most famous evangelist was now in the
starting blocks.

5

NEW LIFE AND NEW MISSION

Festo's new life began immediately by his telling people what God had done for him and asking them for forgiveness. Two boys were converted in his class. His next stop was the market place and then to the town and fields to tell people what had happened to him and to put things right where necessary. He visited his Uncle Karegyesa with whom he used to drink. It was an awkward meeting with his uncle who was not sympathetic to his conversion. He then went to see Rwabugarame, his stepfather, whom he had hated for beating his mother. This was a happier meeting with the two hugging each other. Festo also went to see Gregory Smith, the school supervisor. This was hard for Festo. Part of his antipathy was racial and, besides, he lived fifty miles away. Festo felt the Spirit had said to him, 'Take your bicycle over the weekend and go to see the man. Now that you are liberated he is your brother. Tell him that you love him.' Their meeting was emotional and Gregory Smith became a close friend for decades to come.

Festo began to devour the Bible. He took the words of the Bible literally, as did most of his friends in those days. He turned to prayer and joined daily fellowship meetings after school. These gatherings were filled with a seriousness to hear God speaking. He read books by Oswald Chambers, Andrew Murray and John Wesley's journals. But these books placed a burden on him that he could not at that time handle properly or understand fully regarding 'crucifying the old nature'.

Soon euphoria faded into a form of legalism. Festo began to struggle again because he constantly felt he was guilty on some point or another. One night he turned to prayer and here is his record of that event.

Suddenly I felt as if somebody quietly said to me, 'Festo, how did you come to Me?'

I said, 'Oh I was in bad shape, Lord.'

'And did you find Me lacking to meet all your almost impossible needs?'

'No, Lord, You did it in a minute. You filled my empty heart, You lifted the burden of my sin, You changed my hostility into love, You opened a whole new world to me. It was You alone, by the Holy Spirit when I came to You, Lord. What do You want?'

'You have done everything you can to be perfect and sinless, but you have not turned your focus on Me. As you first received Me, so, in the same way, also walk. There is no other

place you can go than to My death for you on the cross. I am always here and available to deal with anything that the devil throws at you. As long as you are in the flesh, it is at the cross where you will find My power. Where did you get your liberation?'

'At the cross.'

'Go there again and again.'

It was quite a shock. It was as if heaven opened that evening. I saw my struggles ending by simply turning to Him who had always been right there, but whom I had been almost by-passing as if there were another. I wanted to find the key to perfection in order to please Him; but He was the key. My reasoning that I must be perfect because God wants me to be perfect had left out the fact that He is our perfection. In determining to present myself perfect before Jesus, I had been looking for a solution other than by Jesus ... I had got to the position where I knew Jesus had saved me, but now I wanted the secret of being perfect so I could please Him. In doing this I was unconsciously saying that God is not all sufficient.

The lesson that evening brought a tremendous breakthrough. I entered a new stage of my Christian walk with God, where I was no longer working hard to make myself perfect. I was enjoying the finished perfection of someone who died for me. I had learned that a deeper relationship with Jesus Christ was all I needed. I finally realised what Paul was saying when he wrote that we had been crucified with Christ, and that all I had to do was continually to turn to Christ. It was almost like another salvation.

Now Festo embarked on an activity that would at times frustrate his school where he was the most popular teacher, and also the activity which would increasingly dominate his life — evangelism.

He joined teams that went out each weekend to testify in the villages round about. The zeal, urgency and sincerity of these teams were phenomenal. He said, 'I felt people had a right to hear what God had done for me. In some obscure way I felt they had a claim on me to tell them the Gospel' (*Biog.*, p. 113).

Soon the new converts were founding bush churches and the teams spread into the Hinterland, some on foot, others on bicycles. Their team endured many primitive living conditions — often sleeping under the stars, to wake up and spend the entire day preaching in the market place. Festo was a particularly compelling preacher. Hundreds of new converts upset the balance of things in the villages by ignoring the old traditional ways. Festo's Uncle Karegyesa eventually had some arrested and jailed, with Festo pleading with him for their release. He ordered Festo off his property. But one night Karegyesa was awakened by his wife to tell him she had been converted. She immediately began to witness to her experience, much to her husband's disgust.

Festo became engaged to a dignified young teacher named Mera who taught at Kabale girls' boarding school. The wedding would be months later and meantime Festo was transferred to Kigezi High School in Kabale. He became an enthusiastic member of St Peter's Church, now missing the weekend mission trips.

Here he gained for the first time an understanding of some of the wider consequences of the revival on all involved. Joe Church, Lawrence Barham and Gregory Smith helped Festo to understand what had been happening. It was a stormy time for the East African Revival.

Tensions existed between the Keswick-influenced Rwanda Mission and the broader CMS. Those outside the revival refused to believe that the weeping, singing, public confessing and other acts could be caused by the Holy Spirit.

Joe Church accompanied the teams on this mission and the increasing friendship between him and the evangelists was most beneficial. Amongst them in the team was William Nagenda, who became a great preacher in his own right. Festo would often translate for Dr Joe Church and it became evident how talented Festo was at this work. Festo and Joe Church became like brothers. Soon Joe Church also realized how brilliant a preacher Festo was in his own right. Festo had the knack of picture language and making simple Bible stories come alive. Furthermore, his own personal testimony always had an effect. When Festo preached, people were always confronted by the love of God. He was finally invited to be the official interpreter for a convention in the capital Kampala, where he proved to be competent in translating in three languages — Luganda, Swahili and Rukiga.

The revival continued to be burdened with enthusiasm and excess, such as copious weeping and repentance, and great leaping for joy. These actions became viewed as signs of authenticity to prove a person was truly revived. But Festo came to see through these things and later wrote:

The devil is not afraid of people singing and jumping for joy in times of revival! He doesn't say 'stop jumping', because he knows they enjoy it. All he says is 'Jump a little higher' — and the higher you jump the more 'spiritual' you are!

The wind of heaven has come, and people shake. I've seen people fall down. Then the devil comes very easily, and says to people who shook, 'Now to experience the fullness of the power of God you have to shake! If you don't shake, you haven't got it.' So you could find the brethren fighting over whether you should shake, shout, be silent or act in a particular way. But when you try and copy some kind of reaction, you produce a fake.

Festo felt he was freed from what he called 'Revival Rules'. He wanted to enter into full-time evangelism but felt that it was not yet time for that.

On 30 December 1943 Festo Kivengere and Mera were married in St Peter's Church, Rugarama Hall, Kabale. In 1944 their first daughter was born and was baptized with the name of 'Peace'. After the war the demand for education increased. Festo continued to harbour ideas of full-time evangelism but still felt the time was not right.

At the end of 1945 a convention was held to celebrate ten years of revival. Huge crowds attended. After the convention Festo and Mera left for Dodoma in Tanganyika to take up a post there. Festo felt God was calling him there because of reports that the church there was extremely sleepy and dead.

The following years were filled with new experiences. Dodoma was an arid town in central Tanganyika. It felt like the end of the world. The biggest building was the Cathedral of the Holy Spirit built by past CMS missionaries and their converts. Their home was not ready for them. The bush surrounding the town was full of lion and hyena, ticks were plentiful and in addition they had to deal with the superiority of the white missionaries.

Festo and his friend Wakabi engaged in open-air preaching and soon had a small group of converts. But they encountered opposition from the local evangelical church. Besides the local opposition to giving 'testimonies', Festo discovered that in 1939 there had indeed been a revival in Tanganyika accompanied by much weeping, fainting and uncontrollable praying. However, all that had passed and there was now a firm opposition to it starting again. Then their second daughter was born, in 1946. She was named Lydia.

The church leaders could not understand that the people they had baptized, when touched by the revival, would stand up and confess conversion as if it was for the first time. The teams eventually caused the local church council to remove Festo's status as a lay preacher of the church and forbade him to preach in Dodoma again. Festo was learning the dangers of defining who was 'in' with God and who was 'out'! He, Mera and Wakabi and Apofia gave themselves to prayer. They opened their home for meetings which were soon crowded. Yet even these were opposed, with the local church announcing that anyone who attended Festo's home gathering would be excommunicated.

However, other opportunities for ministry soon opened up, with invitations to other centres, and many were converted.

In 1948 Festo and Mera lost their little girl Lydia to cerebral malaria. This very moving story is told in his book *Revolutionary Love* and describes how both he and Mera experienced the presence and help of God. He described his wife's reaction by saying, 'God blessed her soul and Heaven came near her, too.'

As time went on, the opposition against them began to fade. Even the canon of the cathedral publicly testified to his conversion. School work and evangelistic work increased. He began travelling throughout Tanganyika and for seven years his life would be school, home, meetings, lay preaching and evangelistic missions to far-flung places throughout Uganda, Tanganyika and Kenya. Festo became a leader in the revival.

Festo's passion as an evangelist sometimes caused problems. It seems that on occasions there was not enough wisdom to match his zeal. His head teacher, missionary Noel Blythell, recalls that Festo's constant evangelizing caused administrative headaches for the school, as he was always requesting leave of absence to attend conventions or evangelistic missions. He often left behind a very annoyed school staff who had to pick up the slack caused by his absence. He particularly caused problems for Blythell who concluded that he did not want any more evangelists on his teaching staff.

Festo also paid the price in terms of family life. On one occasion he was taking Mera and his daughter back to Uganda for the holidays when he was persuaded to leave them halfway through the difficult journey home, with no help except that of a schoolboy, to go and preach the gospel.

In assessing these occasions one needs to remember how difficult it must have been for the missionaries and for Festo and the revival teams. These missionaries were the ones that brought the gospel to East Africa in the first place. Now that the gospel was believed and preached with fiery zeal it appeared that they were disapproving. On the other hand the missionaries rejoiced in the enthusiasm, zeal and gifts of so many converts but could not always assess what to do about the sheer exuberance of the revival and its impact on the Christians.

But as time went by, there was a steady change in attitude toward the revival. Opposition faded and the movement steadily gained credence. It stressed a daily walk with Christ and a transparent lifestyle — values that were hard to negate. The church in Tanganyika was growing rapidly. Bush churches were all over the place and many, including missionaries, had now begun to be touched by what was happening.

Festo now began to receive invitations ranging from Dar es Salaam, to Rwanda, to Kenya. Furthermore they were from different denominations, from Lutheran to Moravians. His circle of friendships with missionaries also increased. Amongst them was Norman Grubb, son-in-law of C. T. Studd, Roy Hession, author of *The Calvary Road*, and Dr Paul White, who later wrote the famous Jungle Doctor stories.

A new head teacher was appointed to Dodoma, called Max Wiggins. Festo listened to him preach and was greatly impressed with his careful expository sermons. He borrowed some of Wiggins' library and began to understand biblical exposition and theology.

In the years that followed there were great conversions, and wonderful stories from Festo's friend William Nagenda's visit to Angola, India and North America. But in Kenya a new evil force spread abroad — the Mau Mau. The Kikuyu Christians were in a very difficult position. They were expected to join the fight for freedom from the British and were well aware of wrongs committed against the people. They were expected to join the uprising. But to do so required the taking of blood oaths and an agreement to kill. This was the beginning of eight years of life lived on a razor edge with very faithful Christians being tortured and killed. Festo heard many horror stories and tales of extreme bravery which he used in his preaching.

During these years the Kivengere family experienced their own personal upheavals. Festo's grandfather died, and Festo returned home for the funeral. Makobore was not only a king, but in African culture grandparents have a status largely lost in the west. Many attended the funeral, including sub chiefs and British administrators. At his funeral Festo made the following remark.

Makobore was a big, important man, but now he is dead and gone. Jesus died, but now He is alive and will never die again. He is bigger than any other king.

His Uncle Karegyesa, who used to drink with him, asked him afterwards: 'Is this really true? Is Jesus bigger than my father?' 'Yes,' said Festo, and Karegyesa was deeply impressed.

About this time Festo and Mera also had to arrange for their daughter Peace to be put through school back in Kabale. It was a boarding school and young Peace was not impressed with the idea. In 1954 their fifth child was born. Her name was Charity. They now had four daughters (one had died) and no sons. In Africa this would have been thought of as unfortunate, but not for Festo. He said, 'I love my girls — I would never exchange them.'

In his book *Revolutionary Love* he gives a glimpse into this family life.

> Too often, when something goes wrong at home, I turn in on myself and keep quiet, hoping that my wife will not detect it. But she does. Thank God she does.

> We both know that we are grieving the Holy Spirit when we sit on something that is unforgiven. My wife's ministry is a gentle word that turns my eyes away from my misery to see again the pure light of Jesus' face and to kneel down at His cross.

> She knows when I have a problem. She knows when I am hard. She knows when I am depressed and she knows how to help me. Sometimes when I preach she afterwards takes me aside and says, 'Festo, as you were preaching today, you made too much noise. People could not get all the words.'

Or another day she might say, 'Festo, you are wearing a frown. Is there something wrong? Let us go to Jesus together.' I sometimes thank God and am healed. Other times I pull back, well up and begin thinking, 'Am I not the head of this house? Why should she speak to me like that? She is just impossible.'

When that happens, I get more and more puffed up until finally I am like a big balloon. A balloon's emptiness of all but air reminds me of the New Testament word that means 'empty glory'. I am inflated with myself, thinking that the bigger I am the better; I act as if I am saying, 'Now everybody bow down to me!'

I get fussy with the children. They bump into my balloon and it bounces them away. Of course, when the children bounce away they become like balloons too and soon the whole home is full of inflated human beings. In the evening I take my Bible, while I am still inflated, and call the family together for prayers. My wife comes, poor thing; she has been bounced off and is becoming inflated. My children come, resenting me. In that condition, is there any fellowship in our home?

How in the world is the Holy Spirit going to draw this family together? It isn't easy. But in one way or another, using the sharp point of His Word, the Saviour gets ready to prick one of the balloons. My problem is that I think my wife ought to be deflated first, but the Holy Spirit knows better. He is just and good and will deal only with me concerning what is wrong with me, not on what I think is wrong with someone else.

When He pricks a balloon ... whooooosh! One of us truly asks for forgiveness and that balloon is limp, and then others also get tender and approachable and we can relate, communicate, and understand each other again.

You know how the hinges of a door can get rusty, and when someone opens the door, it squeaks. I hear my voice going up and up. This makes the children squeak too. We need oil. When the Spirit of Christ puts His oil on the hinges, our voices are natural again, hearts beating in tune

(*Revolutionary Love*, pp. 57-58).

He often took these illustrations into the pulpit. He told stories always stressing the love of Christ.

At this time ordination was raised by Bishop Alfred Stanway but Festo declined. Although he desperately wanted to be a full-time evangelist he was cautious of ordination, still influenced by the Rwanda Mission's emphasis on the laity.

Much of the preaching by laity at that time consisted of simply telling their stories. But Festo was fiery and dynamic — a great story teller who held people enthralled when he spoke. Although he had no formal theology he nevertheless preached a biblical message. However the missionaries still felt the need to challenge him in regard to some of his statements. Thus their interacting, added to the great amount of reading he did, sharpened his biblical and orthodox views.

There was tremendous spiritual vitality at this time with 'communities of fellowship' keeping in touch with each other in hundreds of villages, towns and cities by letters, travellers, or small gatherings.

One of the battles Festo was embroiled in was a trend he discovered at the Great Kabale Convention in 1955, celebrating the past ten years of the Holy Spirit's activity in East Africa. There was a great hostility by the Protestant churches against the Roman Catholics which later seeped into Ugandan politics. The Roman Catholics considered the revival to be fanatical and even demon-inspired. The Protestants considered the Roman Catholics to be evil and enemies, worse even than the pagans. In a sermon at Kabale Cathedral one Sunday evening Festo addressed the matter, reminding his listeners Christ died for the Roman Catholics as well as others. His sermon caused deep offence and resentment.

The following year, Uncle Karegyesa finally became a Christian and the change in him was staggering. He returned large sums of money he had obtained fraudulently. He asked forgiveness from people he had oppressed and he gave back many head of cattle. Shortly after his conversion he died and Festo preached at his funeral.

Soon after this, Bishop Stanway obtained a bursary for Festo to go to London to study to obtain a diploma in education. However, Mera and the girls needed to return to Uganda so Festo went to London alone.

6

NEW EXPERIENCES

Festo took to London easily. Later his friend William Nagenda joined him and soon the two were in great demand in pulpits all over England. There they met up with Roy Hession and made acquaintances with Richard Bewes who would be an ongoing influence in his life.

Festo went to listen to all the great London preachers including Dr Martyn Lloyd-Jones of Westminster Chapel whom he found very impressive. But his place of worship was All Souls, Langham Place, where he was deeply influenced by John Stott.

By the end of that year Festo had made contact with many Christians across England — what we today would call 'networking'.

His time in London was not without its difficulties, especially homesickness, and back home Mera found the burden of caring for small children a heavy one as money was in short supply. She lived in a guest house prepared by Lilian Clarke and although she struggled she never complained.

On his return in August 1957, Festo was sure God was calling him to full-time service but was not sure how this was to come about.

Uganda was now approaching independence and national politics began to exert its influence. Festo felt his time to move permanently from Dodoma in Tanganyika had come. He was offered the job of assistant school supervisor for Kigezi District but also felt increasingly frustrated because of his deepening sense that he ought to be in full-time evangelism.

He then was invited to join a team of East Africans travelling to Australia where he would act as an interpreter for Bishop Yohana Omari from Tanganyika, who was not fluent in English. The Australian tour would be lengthy and so he resigned his school job with the intention of taking up the new offer when he returned. Altogether they had spent thirteen years in Tanganyika and a trickle of revival had swelled to a great flood during these years through Anglican, Lutheran, Mennonite and Moravian churches.

In Australia the CMS had planned a very busy itinerary. For six months they spoke in churches, youth meetings, summer schools and all manner of conferences and meetings. Omari would begin the meetings by speaking for ten to fifteen minutes, with Festo picking up after him. Festo stood with royal poise, clear speech and oratorical skills. Many people were converted and the meetings were a great success. Festo was persuaded to stay on after the tour and then preached to Aboriginal people accompanied by Dean Lance Shilton. At first there was no result to his preaching and Festo felt quite shaken. However, he did some self-examination and concluded that the problem lay with him. He found he had been preaching with a bias and had created his own barriers. He felt the Lord say to him, 'You just speak to them as My precious people for whom I died and forget everything you have heard about them.' That evening he couldn't stop preaching and a great breakthrough occurred. Festo concluded: 'When once you love people, then you will find ways and means of putting it across.'

Festo finally returned home to his fortieth birthday, a new job and Uganda's independence. He felt really confused about the future and the struggle with the desire to do full-time evangelism continued.

His return to Kabale occurred at the same time as the country was bracing itself for independence. There was a change of attitude towards white people and the ancient hostility between Roman Catholics and Protestants was affecting national politics. Festo worked with Lilian Clarke, working hard to ensure that all 150 schools in their area would be kept up to scratch, both organizationally and financially.

Soon after he returned to Kabale an event occurred which would accelerate the new direction his life was taking: Billy Graham was coming to town. Festo was cautious about this visit. The East African evangelicals did not use big choirs or 'altar calls'. Nor were they used to the organization and administration that a Billy Graham event entailed.

Nevertheless he joined in with other leaders who were helping with preparation for the visit. Then they heard that Billy Graham was to speak in Kenya and an interpreter was needed who would be fluent in Swahili and English. Festo was chosen and he readily agreed.

100,000 people turned up for the meetings held at the foot of Mt Kilimanjaro. Billy Graham had been briefed about Festo and his evangelistic ability and said to him, 'Don't bother to translate literally. You know what I mean — just get that across.' This was a great encouragement to Festo who soon realized that God had a lot for him to learn. He accompanied Billy Graham to some of the villages. On one occasion Billy Graham was faced with a crowd of men who had been drinking and was at a loss at what to preach to them. Festo told him, 'Just talk to them about John 3 v 16 and trust the Lord.' Graham did so with great effect. Festo remembered Graham preaching the same message years later to Cambridge students at Great St Mary's Church with many being converted.

Festo also interpreted for team member Cliff Barrows and stayed with the team for the entire three-week tour. They also preached at a stadium in Burundi. Billy Graham was loved by all and so was his interpreter who was dynamic, simple and clear in what he said. A firm friendship was struck between Billy Graham and Festo Kivengere. Billy Graham commented that 'Festo Kivengere was one of the most spiritual men I have ever known.'

Festo was greatly exhilarated by this experience and it fired up his resolve to get into full-time evangelism as soon as possible. He returned to his school job but continued his evangelistic efforts with his friend William Nagenda. One of the problems they had to deal with in the ensuing months was a faction of the revival which became exclusive, legalistic and super-spiritual. It was all they could do to keep the Christians on track.

Billy Graham's influence continued to reach into Festo's life. He attended a conference in Switzerland to discuss effective evangelism. About forty leaders attended and the meeting was filled with acrimony until Festo stood to his feet and pointed the group back to the person of Jesus.

Later Dr Stephen Olford from New York commented on what happened after Festo's quiet statement: 'Every person in that room was smitten with conviction and a spirit of brokenness. With a word from Billy Graham we were all on our knees and for hours prayers of repentance, brokenness, confession and restoration poured forth from every person in the room. God had met us under the spell and power of one word, "Jesus".'

Back at home Festo became the school supervisor and Lilian Clarke became his assistant. As the march toward independence increased, Festo began to worry about what would happen when the missionary leadership was given over to a small group of ordained African Christians. Although he himself was not ordained he saw the potential problem and had a vision of a future well-run church with able and mature leadership.

Festo's popularity continued to increase and he and his friend William Nagenda were very busy with preaching and conferences. They were conducting an evangelistic mission in Tanganyika (which was to become Tanzania) when they heard that Rwanda and Burundi had fallen into civil strife. Terrible massacres took place, with Christians on both sides being killed. Festo tells the story of a Tutsi friend of his who was captured by Hutu soldiers (*Revolutionary Love*, p. 75).

> He said to the gunmen, 'Before you kill me, may I have permission to say a few things?'
>
> 'Say them quickly.'
>
> 'First,' he said, 'I love you, second, I love my country. Third, I will sing a song.' In their mother tongue he sang all four verses of the hymn which starts: 'Out of my bondage, sorrow and night, Jesus I come'. When he finished, they shot him.

His evangelistic ministry grew both far and wide and he increasingly felt the inner strain between what he was doing — school teaching, and what he felt should occupy him full time — evangelism. He faced the problem of giving up his salary and his house. He talked things over with his family and his friends and all agreed that he should stop teaching, step out in faith and become a full-time evangelist. He responded at the end of 1961. Independence came in 1962 and, were he still a teacher, would probably have been caught up in the affairs of the new state. On his last day in the school office, he left a note on his desk that said, 'Praise the Lord, at last I am free.'

The following years became a flurry of activity as he sorted out the family finances, started travelling to America and experienced God's providential provision financially for himself and his family. He preached at the sixth International Student Missionary Convention at the University of Illinois. His style of preaching was very different, as he spoke in vivid picture language, making Bible stories come to life. It was a very African style of preaching which Festo mastered and adapted to his new audiences.

Festo and Nagenda travelled throughout America, with Festo always the evangelist. Everywhere people were greatly moved by their stories of the revival in Africa and they operated together like brothers.

Stephen Olford tells of a visit to his church made by the two men. They spoke at his Wednesday night Bible study and prayer meeting.

> *These two dear servants of God approached the pulpit together, and in tandem fashion taught and testified concerning the work of the Holy Spirit in revival, illustrating lucidly what was taking place in Rwanda and Uganda. The power of the Holy Spirit was so evident in the hour that followed that there was hardly a dry eye in the congregation. As the great themes of brokenness, confession of sin, walking in the light, being filled with the Spirit, and living out the glories of the blessed Saviour were emphasised and applied, my own heart was deeply moved in repentance and response to the call of Christ to another quality of life.*

Festo was ushered into the world of full-time evangelism. The reader should remember that at this stage in his life he still had no formal theological training. His preaching was simple and graphic. His preparation was prayer, meditation, and a few notes on a subject or Bible passage. When he sat on a platform before thousands of sophisticated people he would sometimes panic. 'I'd pray and tell the Lord, "My notes and my thoughts on this text are still not co-ordinated." Then the devil would step in and accuse me, "Is it going to make sense? Haven't you been lazy? Did you pray properly? You were careless!"' Yet when he stood up to speak he would plunge right in and audiences felt, when he had finished, that Jesus really loved them. He once told a friend that he felt western Christians needed 'a fresh presence of the love of the Risen Christ'.

Festo also felt being an African was a great advantage in worldwide ministry. He would say things a white preacher would not get away with and he was not in competition with anybody. He now began to get invited to other countries, with conferences in Switzerland, England, India, and back home for Uganda's Independence on 9 October 1962.

Milton Obote of the United People's Congress became the new prime minister and he had a tough job ahead of him. Colonial rule had created a lot of problems for Uganda's new leaders and for a long time there would be continued reliance on Britain and other countries to support their independence. In addition the tensions between Roman Catholics and Protestants were continuing and now there were huge problems produced by the terrible Rwandan massacres. It should be noted that these terrible massacres occurred before the infamous 1994/5 massacres in Rwanda.

Festo continued his evangelistic activities. He was well known and increasingly respected and in huge demand. Yet his family paid the price for his long absences. His family life became fragmented. Mera and the girls experienced great loneliness. Mera sometimes struggled with bitterness that she had been left alone so much, yet she won her own battles and always supported his ministry. He was born to preach and so the family accepted it. Festo acknowledged her support and paid tribute to her for the way she raised the children, and the way eventually opened for his two daughters, Peace and Joy, to study in London.

But overseas travel had made another impression on Festo. He began to see that there was a difference between lay people and ordained people when it came to having influence. Ordination could open doors that a layman could not open. This was an interesting development. In many western circles today the drift is towards a more independent laissez-faire approach to ministry. Nevertheless even now many missionaries apply for ordination because of the acceptability it brings in some cultures or situations. It is also true that in yet other cultures a preferred qualification in a field other than theology would open doors more quickly.

He had been offered a scholarship to the Pittsburgh Seminary. This was a three-year course leading to ordination and Festo decided to accept it. His decision had a mixed reception back home but finally all was in place. His plans dovetailed nicely with the fact that he had been able to have the first home he ever owned, built with the help of funds from his overseas friends. Mera and his family moved in. She had found a job at the Hornby High School for Girls. Peace and Joy were in England, Hope was at school and Charity was at home. After a sad farewell Festo left for Pittsburgh. He was forty-three years old — a fairly late start for both formal study and ordination to the Anglican ministry.

7

A NEW BEGINNING

Festo's years at Pittsburgh were the start of a new era. He had no sooner arrived in the United States when he began preaching. But in addition he was engulfed with reading, term papers and essays. He admitted that starting study at forty-four was harder than he expected but he ploughed on. He was in great demand as a speaker and quickly began to enjoy life in America.

He was asked to talk about revival but felt cautious about it.

Many people have asked me to speak about revival and I have never really felt comfortable — because then you get into giving people well-worked techniques of how you get a church or community revived: 'What do you do? etc.' That has never been what I call the key to revival. To me, as I look back on the team which was used to bring revival to Kabale in the 1930s, what did they teach? They taught us nothing about techniques, they just stood there like the apostle in Jerusalem and proclaimed the gospel. The facts

> *of sinning, of judgement, of redemption. It just poured out of their burning hearts. Now they didn't meet with tremendous success immediately — in fact, far from it. But I shall never forget what they left behind — Jesus Christ. They preached Jesus Christ and him crucified. Sin was made sinful, judgement was made inevitable, and redemption was the only door. They went, but we were left with something unshakable, and they didn't once mention the word revival to us. Just that the Holy Spirit was with us ... many of us really didn't understand but everybody in the church felt God was there*

(*Biog.*, pp. 234-5).

He managed to make a trip home to preach at the Kabale Convention and also to make plans to bring Mera and the girls back with him.

Two events were unfolding at that time. The first was that the new independent government in Uganda was in decline, and amongst the Christians the charismatic movement with its emphasis on tongues was on the rise. This caused some controversy, especially in regard to the display of emotion, but Festo always maintained that while the revivals did not despise manifestations, real revival is Jesus Christ himself.

Festo never adopted the western style of carefully constructed sermons. Rather, as Richard Bewes commented: 'The message came at you like a child throwing paint with his fingers all at once on a canvas with great excellence.'

But Festo did feel that under all his new influences he was losing his freshness in communicating with his African brothers. He made a decision which he describes as, 'I must be careful not to lose my understanding of the African way of communicating. I made up my mind that Western influence should help to clarify my thoughts, but not force me into a set mould.' This decision made Festo feel more relaxed before his meeting anywhere.

He finally graduated from Pittsburgh Theological Seminary (a Presbyterian college) and was ordained to the order of deacon on 11 June 1966 at St Stephens's Church, Sewickley, Pennsylvania.

This was a landmark day for Festo. It marked the end of his independent ministry and he now became a minister within the Anglican communion. He changed from being a popular evangelist of the revival and became an international evangelist in his own right and on a more formal basis. Festo had a new vision which he put into a letter in America before he left for home.

> While at Pittsburgh Theological Seminary, my wife and I have been laying before the Lord, who called us into His blessed service more than twenty years ago, the fact of where in His great vineyard back in Africa He wants us to serve, and in which way.
>
> It is through these times of heart-searching, desiring to know His will for us, that the idea of working on an interdenominational basis for the mobilization of African evangelists into a united force for God wherever they are, began taking shape in our hearts

(p. 243).

Then he continued to share his practical needs in his letter
— need for a home, a car, a fixed salary for the sake of his
long-suffering family, an office and a secretary. Several
churches responded most generously.

While Festo finished up in America with a very busy
schedule, other events were unfolding back in Uganda.
Richard Lyth had been consecrated as the first bishop of the
newly formed Kigezi diocese. Erica Sabiti had become the
first African Archbishop of Uganda, Rwanda and Burundi.
Dr Milton Obote had become the first executive head of the
Ugandan Republic while Festo was away, but in the political
turmoil that followed he called in the help of a member of
an insignificant tribe near the Sudanese border. He was a
professional soldier, a huge man, whose name was Idi Amin.
He led brutal raids on the Kabaka tribe and when Festo
arrived home the country was in a political crisis.

Festo was due to be ordained on 17 December 1967 but his
diary was so booked up with evangelistic commitments that
if he stayed for the ordination he would miss certain strategic
opportunities abroad. The result was that in consultation
with Bishop Lyth, Festo was ordained a presbyter a week
earlier in a two-hour service on Sunday 10 December before
a packed cathedral.

Festo was now an ordained clergyman in the Church
of Uganda. Dick Lyth was his Bishop and Erica Sabiti
Archbishop. A minister for the north of the country was
the Provincial Secretary. His name was Janani Luwum, who
would later play a huge role in the unfolding events of the
life of Festo, the Ugandan Church and Ugandan politics.

And so the stage was set for a major confrontation later with Idi Amin, but for the moment Festo was starting the rest of his life's ministry. He packed a suitcase and boarded a plane.

His fame as a preacher increased and some began calling him the 'Billy Graham of Africa'. He was a truly gifted evangelist. He was personally poised, always smartly dressed and appeared to the African people with whom he ministered as very impressive. His preaching was based on a story-telling method which was becoming legendary. He was offered a job with World Vision which he turned down because of his belief that he needed to stay with his diocese as a home base while he preached abroad as much as his time permitted.

Immediately, he was invaded with calls to preach at evangelistic missions, conferences, retreats, rallies and services for a number of denominations. He visited New Guinea, Israel, Switzerland, New York, as well as the little bush churches in the villages of his own home territory of Kigezi. He was burning to speak of Christ and his great stamina enabled him to cope with the rigours of travelling, besides which he felt at ease when preaching. He stayed at hotels rather than private homes to conserve his strength and when he was in Africa was able to translate in up to five languages.

As far as preaching is concerned in the 1950s and 1960s his friend William Nagenda had become widely known as the strongest preacher in Uganda. But now that opinion shifted to Festo. Festo used words and images no one else would. For instance he described non-Christian people as 'squeaky hinges', conversion was described as the time when

Christ came into one's life as 'soothing oil'. Festo also now
introduced more content into his Bible teaching. He said,
'Without Christ, preaching is a dry exercise. The Bible does
not speak and words do not come' (*Biog.*, p. 258). He once
gave an illustration of preaching as follows:

> *Take a piece of metal; it is colourless, dull, cold, nothing
> attractive about it. But put it into the fire. Let the fire run
> through it. It will get warm. It loses its rough surface, its
> hardness, its colourlessness. It begins to glow. You begin to
> see glory, not the glory of the metal, but of the fire in the
> metal.*

He also remarked:

> *Sometimes I see people responding to the word of the Lord
> which I have preached, even if my heart is not quite right.
> But I don't get away with self-congratulations, and neither
> did Moses. God took Moses aside as a friend, had some
> fellowship with him, and told him a few things that had
> gone wrong between them. He loves me that way too. No
> matter what grace has done for me in the past, I still need to
> experience daily the power of the cleansing blood of Jesus…
> And that is not easy.*

He lived with a keen sense of his own need for continual
repentance. 'In and of myself, I can't be real. It frightens
me. It embarrasses me. But when I go down to the foot of
the cross and meet Jesus there, His grace covers my sins,
forgives my weaknesses, and allows me to be what I am — a
forgiven man.'

He also discovered that repentance is not easy and used a homely illustration to clarify the difficulty.

> *It is easy to cause a wound, but hard to heal it. If God did not intervene, with grace, we would all be reckoned as murderers. One day I used an expression that cut the heart of my dear wife and caused a wound there.*
>
> *In the atmosphere of mutual forgiveness, and in the provision that Jesus Christ has made for us, Mera and I have discovered that through self-forgetting and self-sacrificing is born a truly creative love. Instead of one emptying the other person for one's own need, each fulfils the other, making him or her more of a person, having more dignity. It brings out the latent qualities in the other, and it partakes somewhat of the love of Christ, who loves His Bride into perfection.*

Meantime around the world history continued to unfold. In 1968 Dr Martin Luther King, the American civil rights leader, was assassinated. This greatly angered and saddened Kivengere. But earlier, in 1961, another event had occurred which was virtually going to affect Kivengere's life from then on. He met Michael Cassidy.

Cassidy was born in Johannesburg. He was a white and privileged South African who was converted at Cambridge and soon had the idea of having evangelistic teams spread out across Africa. Cassidy developed a burden for the lonely, lost, dispossessed of a swiftly changing Africa. At Fuller Seminary he began to clarify his vision for Africa and it was while he was there that he first heard Kivengere speak. Festo was travelling with his famous Uganda Revival exponent, William Nagenda. Michael well remembers Festo's electrifying talk on 'The little foxes that spoil the vines' (from Song of Solomon 2:15). Festo was expounding on how it is the little sins and little failures of life which can finally add up to spoiling our whole testimony and walk with the Lord.

While he was at Fuller Seminary, Cassidy established Africa Enterprise (AE), later to be known in East Africa as African Evangelistic Enterprise (AEE), which established more clearly in the East African context the nature of the enterprise. This was necessary as in East Africa there were already several other commercial ventures known as African Enterprise. However elsewhere across the world and even in southern and west Africa, the ministry was known as African Enterprise. Michael soon had a board and an office in Pasadena and later established many other support offices in other parts of the world.

Cassidy was a gifted evangelist and a strong leader. He was deeply committed to working with an interdenominational team seeking not only to evangelize but also to bring reconciliation and healing to those formally polarized by racism and tribal or ethnic differences. Cassidy also always visualized in African Enterprise strong dimensions of socio-political concern, practical action and compassionate care to accompany the clear preaching of the gospel.

Cassidy had ongoing deep spiritual experiences at Fuller in which God drew very near to him and expanded his vision for Africa. He began praying round the continent for a major capital city each day of thirty-one days of the month. A continent-wide vision was developing. Then in 1961 along with a friend he toured the whole of the African continent during the northern summer and travelled some 50,000 kilometres beginning with Tripoli and Libya, Tunis and Tunisia, Algiers in Algeria and then all the way round the African continent. This experience confirmed in his heart and mind that AE was to be a continent-wide ministry. The logic of having another team based in East Africa, and not just a team in South Africa, was compelling.

Then in 1968 Cassidy found himself ministering at the West African congress on evangelism in Ibadan, Nigeria. Festo Kivengere was another speaker there. After hearing Festo deliver an extraordinary message on the story of the East African Revival and its origins, commitments and emphasis, Cassidy went back to his room very moved and sobered. As he prayed, there came an overwhelming conviction that the Lord was speaking to him: 'You must build another African Enterprise team around Festo.' Cassidy immediately rushed to Festo's room, and excitedly burst in saying to him: 'Brother Festo, I believe the Lord has just spoken to me and said that we in African Enterprise need to build another African team around you.' Festo looked at Cassidy with a mix of mystification, excitement and caution. Cassidy told how AE had been invited by the combined churches of Nairobi to do a major city-wide campaign beginning later that year and extending into 1969. It would be so wonderful if Festo could join in the endeavour and the two men could team up together for the preaching side of things. It had been a notion already in the minds of the Nairobi committee. In the Nairobi venture, suggested Cassidy, they could test the waters, as it were, and see if the Lord confirmed that they were meant to work together.

This was a mind-blowing idea. Festo was an internationally renowned spokesman for the revival. He seemed unmoved at an initial overture made to him. He already had an international ministry. He was constantly preaching throughout Africa as well as in countries worldwide. He saw no point in starting another organization.

But in addition to that, Michael Cassidy and the AEE team were South African. In those days when apartheid ruled South Africa with all of its attendant injustices, South African whites were anathema. Festo felt that to link up with a white South African could jeopardize his own ministry in Africa. His ministry was his life. He wanted nothing to detract from it.

But Festo could not simply dismiss Michael and he continued to pray about the matter and finally came to understand Michael as another African taking a stand against all that dehumanized black Africans in South Africa and beyond.

After much prayer and reflection, Festo committed himself to preaching with Michael at the citywide Nairobi Crossroads Mission at the end of 1968 and on into 1969. And then for the rest of that year he carried on with his hectic programme of conferences, retreats, conventions and rallies. His vitality, stamina and single-mindedness for evangelism was legendary. As his fame grew, so did the stories about his unusual and unconventional style. His family also experienced the stresses of having a well-known husband and father who was in great demand.

When he finally got to preach with Cassidy in Nairobi, they adopted a tandem preaching style. Festo spoke in Swahili and an American Mennonite Bishop, Don Jacobs, interpreted for him; Michael then spoke English and somebody translated for him into Swahili. The response to the gospel invitations was huge.

After the mission, which ran for some eight months and which had a huge impact, Festo returned to Kampala, Uganda. Obote was in charge of Uganda at that time and the situation was fast unravelling. Festo was becoming increasingly concerned for his country but the challenge of the wide Africa remained with him. Not long after he was back in Uganda, Cassidy and another AE colleague, Chris Smith, went up to Kampala. Festo had said that he and his wife Mera would be praying about the African Enterprise possibility. Not surprisingly there were all sort of options before him, including an invitation to join the Billy Graham team and be Dr Graham's chief African evangelist in Africa. Another enormous opportunity was on offer from World Vision. There were probably others. Finally in a hotel in Kampala and over lunch when the three men were together came the momentous response from Festo which was to change both his and Cassidy's lives irrevocably. 'Michael,' Festo said with emotion and deep seriousness, 'Mera and I have been praying about the offer and invitation you have made. And we feel the Lord is leading us to join you and work together. African Enterprise is an indigenous African ministry and we really need to be based and housed in such a ministry rather than in one based overseas.' After this extraordinary and emotionally charged conversation, the three men prayed and parted. Cassidy and Smith went back to their room, got on their knees and an overjoyed and ecstatic Cassidy wept tears of gratitude before God.

The ramifications of Festo's agreement meant that the African Enterprise partnership had taken a major and monumental step forward. It was now genuinely a Pan African ministry.

Festo later explained and outlined his reasons why he felt he could accept AE's offer, rather than the many larger American organizations anxious to take him on board. Festo said he was proud to be African and part of the revival. If he was going to join with anybody on a more formal basis it should bear the stamp 'made in Africa' on it. Although African Enterprise had many overseas links it was still African at grassroots. He felt that the Lord required it of him to join up with Cassidy even though the potential for trouble and disruption in his own ministry was real because of its strong link to a white South African.

Festo became the assistant chaplain to the cathedral at Kampala. But soon he was on the move again to various evangelistic meetings.

In Uganda two disputes continued to bubble. The visit of the pope in 1969 raised the furious debate over the acceptability or otherwise of Catholics to the Christians of the revival.

Then a group of the 'awakened' ones, that is some who had been involved in the revival, began a debate about who was truly a Christian. This group became exclusivist, legalistic and racist. For instance, no white missionary was really a Christian and any Africans who travelled overseas inevitably lost their faith because there were no Christians overseas. Dress rules were introduced and Festo became steadily drawn into the controversy by its leader — a certain Mr Mondo.

This became a long drawn-out dispute carried on between many travels, conventions, missions and other meetings both overseas and locally, and added to the stresses Festo already carried.

To add to the tension Obote and Amin were now beginning to fall out. Idi Amin was recruiting a private army and a time bomb was lit in Uganda.

8

A BUSY LIFE

Festo's life was caught up with local duties and overseas invitations — all competing with his responsibilities to his own family.

His first joint travelling experiences of ministry with Michael Cassidy, following the Nairobi Mission, took place towards the end of 1970 and after Michael and the AE team in South Africa had conducted the huge Mission 70 to Johannesburg with 300 churches participating. But after this mission Cassidy and Kivengere were together for an extensive ministry tour across the United States. They began on the East Coast and headed to the West Coast, preaching in a variety of churches and towns and cities of all sizes.

On this tour the two men got to know and understand each other and their separate personalities. They both had one passion — to preach the gospel to others and to convey the message of the East African Revival especially in terms of its focus on the cross and what was termed 'Calvary Love'. As the two men and their wives travelled across the US, they found a combined and shared message very clearly emerging in terms of 'the ministry of reconciliation' as referred to in 2 Corinthians 5. Again and again they expounded that passage and focused in on the notion that 'God has given us the ministry of reconciliation.' In reality they were personifying their message. After all, Festo was black, and Cassidy was white. Festo was more senior and Cassidy was younger. Cassidy was a layman, and Festo destined to be a prominent churchman. Festo came from independent Africa and Cassidy from apartheid South Africa. Not surprisingly their message made an enormous impact all across the US.

It was a learning curve for Festo who up until now had acted largely as a law unto himself. On this tour Michael's wife Carol lost the baby she was carrying and the grief that followed seemed to open Festo up on a more personal level than at any other time on the trip. Then their trip ended, Cassidy went back to South Africa and Kivengere to Uganda.

But not for long. Soon he was on the move again. But his travels took place against the background of a government that was unravelling. Obote had become very unpopular. His regime was beginning to cause chaos and there were now thousands of political prisoners.

Festo heard of the military coup in his country over the radio. Major General (Big Daddy) Idi Amin Dada had seized control of the country. President Obote was out of the country and would return only at risk to his life. Everybody, including Festo, was relieved that Obote had gone.

Amin was immensely popular in the first few weeks. He professed to want the support of the churches and urged all Ugandans to be faithful in their church or mosque — even though he himself was a Muslim. Michael Cassidy flew to Uganda to help Festo set up an African Evangelistic Enterprise board. This proved to be more difficult than at first thought but eventually a Ugandan board was launched, if not an East African board. Lilian Clarke was approached to run the board as executive secretary.

Meanwhile Amin became increasingly erratic and a threat to any form of stability. He established the State Research Bureau with 'agents' who were thugs and killer squads, aided by all the modern technology available at that time. Through all this Festo and other leaders had their job to do. Festo's constant theme was 'the cross'.

> The cross speaks of life in conflict with death, life defeating death... The cross is ... God moving in love to meet violent men and women, Himself facing violence and suffering for us... Your faith was born in violence. The Christian is not scared when nations are upset, when the whole world is shaking. Your faith was born on Calvary — it can stand anything. It is an all-weather faith.

Nevertheless he continued his hectic pace with missions both local and overseas. Even the growing fear of Amin did not prevent some amongst the 'Awakened' from breaking away into a subculture of the revival. But they eventually simply dwindled away.

There arose then a dispute between the different dioceses in Uganda over where the archbishop should be located.

To everyone's amazement Amin himself intervened. He declared that he did not want a divided church in his country and called all bishops and diocesan councils to a meeting at Kampala's Conference Centre to sort matters out.

Festo described it:

> For two days we sat and looked at one another, and the differences remained. But on 28th November, the Lord gave us a message from Philippians. We saw that we were men going up, each one thinking about his reputation and demanding his rights. But that day we caught a vision of the man-coming-down; Jesus, 'who though he was in the form of God, emptied himself, taking the form of a servant...' (Phil. 2: 6-7).

What a change he made! In the presence of 'him who came down' our dear archbishop, Erica Sabiti, and each of the nine diocesan bishops, went down in confession of the sins which had contributed to the divisions in the church and a great melting by the Holy Spirit came upon us all.'

For years afterwards President Amin reminded the bishops that he had 'saved the church.'

The AEE teams meantime now had invitations not only from Africa but all over the world. For the South African and East African teams apartheid was always in the background and tension could erupt quite easily. Michael and Festo were very different people in regard to organizational matters. Festo was more laid back and relaxed. He let others do the organizing and just required a day's warning before a meeting began.

Michael was amenable to team life, and a natural team player who operated a collegial and consensual leadership style. Festo on the other hand, as one Christian leader in England put it, 'came from the land of the kings in Uganda' and therefore did not take kindly to being crossed, challenged or even questioned. Thus there were some painful encounters between the two men. Cassidy felt that he made more apologies and sought forgiveness more often, but that Festo in a strange sort of way found this very difficult and was better at preaching the principle of 'walking in the light' than actually practising it within the African Enterprise team fellowship. While Festo preached openness and brokenness he seemed to find this more difficult in practice. Possibly the tension of working with a white South African played a role. Cassidy commented:

> Festo was not always spontaneous with me. But I found that if I shared something difficult openly with him, it would sometimes illicit a similar response from him. But he was reluctant voluntarily to make himself vulnerable. He could be quite self-protective. Even so, our friendship became very deep and meaningful and something both of us treasured.

The two men, however, learnt much from each other in the way they individually and then together coped with the stress of missions and the handling of thousands of people. In preaching, although both were powerful, nevertheless, they differed somewhat both in preparation and approach. Michael always spoke from very full and carefully constructed notes so that his messages came through as thoughtful and incisive. Festo, on the other hand, while he always prepared thoroughly, relied more on broad sermon outlines which often contained good quotes from significant scholars, but all of these he used as springboards for endless streams of stories and anecdotes which came to his mind out of the very rich experience and background of the revival movement. Said Michael:

> Festo seemed to have an extraordinary genius in seeing a double or even subterranean meaning in a text, so that the surface statements became pretexts and pictures of other meanings which could be brought forth out of the biblical stories.

He added:

> It surprised me often how he would extemporise to such an amazing degree. One verse would trigger off an astonishing flow of material and insights. It was brilliant, sparkling and effervescent. And also filled with lots of fun and humour, in spite of the message being so basically steeped in theology and the Bible and anointed by the Holy Spirit.

Michael often felt, when listening to Festo, that the Hebrew and the African way of looking at things were very similar.

> The Hebrews saw things in pictures. They wrote about them in pictures ... they saw the world as something dynamic, speaking... Festo had the amazing capacity to see the Word of God at both the immediate level and also the subterranean, picture level. He always saw the picture beyond. For example, in the story of Zacchaeus coming down from the tree, Festo told of our need to 'come down', to humble ourselves if we are to find Jesus. And when he told

the story of the disciples rowing on the lake in the storm, he found in it parallels to 'our struggle with life, being battered without Jesus'. He was extremely vivid — you could see your own life and spiritual walk in terms of a vivid picture there in the Bible, which he had just expounded so beautifully.

Many of us have other dimensions to our lives than our ministries, but for Festo, that was it: evangelism was the air he breathed, the food he ate.

Yet Festo was often to be seen reading heavy German theological books which provided him with much stimulation.

Dr Don Jacobs, a leader in AEE, recalled an early meeting of the South African and the East African teams in Switzerland. The meetings were characterized by distrust and tension. Then Festo took a turn to open a session. He began with a testimony. He said he had been praying and expressing his love for Christ when he felt an unmistakable inner voice saying to him, 'I know you love Christ, but do you love Michael?' Don Jacobs recalled:

Having given us his witness, Festo crossed the room and embraced Michael before all of us. This was a moment which had about it the aura of eternity. The fellowship between the South African and East African teams was built upon that little walk of ten steps that Festo took toward Michael. Michael, of course, responded in the spirit, and there was great joy as the Holy Spirit melted the barriers which were separating these teams.

Meanwhile terror was increasing under Amin even though the churches were still under the influence of the revival. In fact the churches were bursting and filled with enthusiasm. It was not surprising that excesses and misunderstandings crept in as they had done in the past. Festo had to deal with this as well as keep up his international meetings. Revivals can be dangerous times. There were wonderful blessings sometimes followed by division, which easily occurred amongst people who were fired up.

In 1972 after one of his trips Festo returned to Uganda to be faced with dreadful news. More mass slaughters had taken place.

It was quite bizarre then, when Amin gave an order that Festo and several others were to accompany the chief army chaplain to preach at army barracks throughout the country. Amin told them to talk as long as they liked and furthermore all soldiers had to attend, Catholics, Protestants and others.

These were amazing scenes with many conversions and a demonstration of the presence of the Holy Spirit. Despite the worsening political scene, and the terrible war with Burundi that year — Festo concentrated on building the ministry of AEE which was now beginning to capture people's interest.

In May 1972 an event occurred which would have far-reaching effects for Kivengere and his work. Bishop Dick Lyth was retiring from his role at Kigezi diocese and a new bishop had to be sought. Festo was the obvious choice and an approach was made to him. Festo saw immediately the advantages for his work in Uganda and surrounds but he would not abandon his work as an evangelist. He made this plain to the delegation that came to see him; but he did not at first tell Michael Cassidy about this. However, when he did share it, Michael was overwhelmed with concern and the AE team in the South, plus others in some of the support boards around the world, were appalled at the potential conflicts of interest. Their teams were very stretched already. They could barely cope and while it was a great honour to support him as bishop it made no sense to Cassidy because no one could envision how he was going to cope with the diocese and the shared leadership of a para-church organization.

However, in Festo's mind, evangelism was considered a duty and a privilege for everyone, and the notion of a bishop who was not an evangelist would have seemed strange to all the revival brethren in the Ugandan context. The enormous stresses of his role as bishop in Kigezi, plus his international travels with all its attendant possibilities, were not comprehensible or conceivable to anyone outside Uganda at that time. But for Festo's fellow believers in Uganda, having a bishop of Festo's international status and carrying out AE ministries at the same time, only served to enhance him in their minds. Thus was Festo eventually elected to succeed Dick Lyth and he accepted the appointment willingly.

In fact it was remarkable how Festo did in reality keep these two balls in the air, although inevitably one or other of his major areas of responsibility was bound to suffer. But if anyone was going to be able to manage it, it was Festo!

Thus as he continued with his travels he went to assorted conventions, for example the Keswick Convention in England, where he became reacquainted with John Stott. In the background Uganda was going through a great deal under Idi Amin, and Festo was conscious of what his people and his church were going through.

Back in Dodoma in Tanzania, 20,000 people attended a convention, but many from Uganda were prevented from attending and imprisoned. The Amin government was scared of collusion between Tanzania and dissident people within Uganda. President Nyerere himself spoke at the convention and was welcomed by Festo.

Then he went back to Europe again only to return to Uganda to more of Amin's madness. 50,000 British Asians had been expelled. Amin became increasingly violent. An abortive attempt at a coup from Ugandans who operated from the Tanzanian side of the border incensed Amin. As his insecurity grew, widespread murder increased. Christians who had helped the former government were targeted and many fled the country.

Meantime plans went ahead for Festo's consecration in Namirembe Cathedral, Kampala, followed by his enthronement a few weeks later, on 3 December 1974, at St Peter's Cathedral, in Kabale. Thousands of people arrived by car, bus or on foot. Hotels were full, as were the homes of many Christians.

The three-and-a-half-hour service commenced at 10.00am. A packed cathedral watched Archbishop Sabiti consecrate

Festo as the new Bishop of Kigezi. It was a momentous occasion. Great festivities took place until late. Bishop Lyth handed the diocese over to Festo and this was his later comment:

> I reminded him that though a man might be ordained, and after serving a curacy in a parish, might be led to minister in schools, prisons, hospitals, industry, etc., a man was consecrated as bishop to be the pastor of his flock, and it was his duty and responsibility to give himself fully and unstintingly to the care of that flock. It has to be said in honesty that Festo failed largely to do this, and inevitably caused resentment among his fellow bishops and many of his diocesan clergy and people.

The huge welcome for him included many foreign guests — evangelists, bishops from Europe, USA, East Africa, Australia and the UK. The services were packed out with much rejoicing. It was a happy time of spiritual refreshment before the storm which was to come.

9

THE LAST KING OF SCOTLAND

I di Amin Dada was born in 1925 and died in Saudi Arabia in 2003. He was a member of the Kakwa ethnic group which converted from Roman Catholicism to Islam in 1910. He left school with a fourth grade education and was recruited to the army by a British colonial army officer.

He became one of the first two Ugandans to become commissioned officers. He was a big and athletic man (6 ft 4 in, or 193 cm), excelling at boxing, swimming and rugby.

Prime Minister Milton Obote saw his rule declining in the wake of several scandals and promoted Amin to colonel and army commander. Amin forced the king of the Buganda people into exile and began recruiting members of ethnic groups from the west and middle area — all with allegiance to him. He seized power from Obote in a military coup on 25 January 1971 to the acclaim of cheering crowds wanting relief from oppression. Interestingly enough, Michael and Carol Cassidy, while on some sabbatical leave in Kenya, went up to Uganda shortly after Amin's coup and were even at a church memorial service for the early martyrs of Uganda which President Idi Amin attended. Commented Michael:

He cut an imposing figure in his military uniform and spoke warmly of the Christian contribution in Uganda. In fact at that point Christians were seeing him as some sort of contemporary Cyrus of Persia who was destined to bless the people of God. How wrong they were!

In any event, Amin started off well but soon established his own brand of dictatorship with severe brutality. Massacres took place, people disappeared, Asians were expelled and members of other ethnic groups, religious leaders, journalists, senior bureaucrats, judges, lawyers, students and intellectuals, all became victims. An atmosphere of violence soon gripped the land.

He came across publicly as a buffoon. In 1976 Amin declared himself the 'uncrowned King of Scotland' and sometimes treated his guests to Scottish accordion music while dressed in Scottish kilts. He finally titled himself, 'HIS EXCELLENCY, PRESIDENT FOR LIFE, FIELD MARSHALL AL HADJI DOCTOR IDI AMIN DADA, VC, CONQUEROR OF THE BRITISH EMPIRE IN AFRICA IN GENERAL AND UGANDA IN PARTICULAR'. And, as mentioned, he sometimes argued that he was the last king of Scotland.

In addition to his erratic, brutal and unpredictable behaviour he was a deadly enemy of the church. His ridiculous posturing may have given rise to cartoons in the west but those living in Uganda lived with the presence of death and evil.

Meanwhile the new Bishop of Kigezi tackled his job with all the enthusiasm of the evangelist. Festo had a clear vision for his five-year-old diocese. His first priority was that the diocese should expand its programme for evangelism as quickly as possible. His biographer writes at this point:

> It is worth noting that Bishop Festo never encountered the conflict of some African Christians, who rejected what the early missionaries had taught — that the religions of Africa were no more than a mass of superstitions, taboos, and magic. Instead they believed African theologians could glean from the vastness of African religions many valuable truths.

> But Bishop Festo never looked back to traditional African religion or beliefs as aids by which to build an African Christianity. He never saw the Christianity that the missionaries had brought to Kigezi as English and therefore needing reinterpretation. Rather, he believed that the Holy Spirit, in reaching out to Uganda, had sent the English Christians so that they might bear witness to Christ. The English were just the conductors of the Gospel, in no way the owners of it. As Festo wrote... 'It is God's work ... when Christ becomes a living risen Lord in the life of a believer...' And when this happened, the believer didn't think about whether it was an African Christianity or an English Christianity. Rather, he thought about what Christ personally wanted of him.

'Go back to a village a week after a man comes to the Lord.
The whole village knows... He has paid his debts... He has
gone to people he hated and said, "I'm sorry". He's now
telling them what Christ means to him. He has carried his
new belief into his business practices. It isn't something he
sits on as a comfortable experience. Christ was at the centre.
And the word was not just read; it was obeyed.'

His second great priority was the development in education
and medical care his diocese needed. In this he was very
successful. He raised the standard of education for the clergy
and raised scholarships in America for his men, especially
with the help of the Billy Graham Association. He also
hoped for more education of the laity but that would have to
wait. Festo was able over the years to obtain doctors, nurses,
agriculturalists, secretaries, teachers and engineers, as well
as the necessary vehicles for them to do their job.

He stressed practical things like responsible stewardship
and proper bookkeeping, and also started to raise money
for a new cathedral for Kabale. He determined to tap into
the resources of generous Western organizations and never
saw that as a problem.

The response to Festo was always sympathetic and
spontaneous and it is worthwhile asking why he found it so
relatively easy to raise money from others. The answer seems
to lie with his own personal qualities. He had a genuine
personal godliness which disarmed people. Furthermore
he appeared to genuinely love people and care for them,
especially the poor in his own diocese. There was a humility
about him that won people over and in addition he had a

natural self-confidence and poise that made people believe in what he was doing. He also appeared to be a good judge of character and of other people's capabilities, and was enthusiastic in developing them.

Sometimes his optimistic approach to people could blind him to real problems with difficult people. But Festo's attitude was always one of acceptance if there had been confession and repentance. Festo himself was an optimist who always bounced back. He spent his days in his diocese in a blur — boards, councils, long mountainous roads, visiting pastors, confirmations and so on. His energy and stamina were legendary. Yet even as his diocese flourished spiritually, the political shadows were growing long.

It became known that Amin had a hit list of 2,000 prominent people he wanted killed — academics, businessmen, church leaders, government officials and others. Then squads of assassins had been mobilized — largely Nubians from the secret police. Stories of the most horrible tortures leaked out of grim brutality, with people beaten or carved up. Some were made to eat their own carved-off flesh, bleeding, and left to die. Stories emerged of government cars with human legs protruding from their boots, and bodies lying rotting in the streets as Amin's power became absolute in Uganda. How accurate all these stories were, only those who suffered through it will know. But it was an indication of the kind of human monster ruling Uganda at that time. He went to the lengths of replacing his cabinet with Muslim military men.

About this time Amin announced on the radio that a number of men had been arrested for subversive activities. They were to be executed in their home communities as a warning to others. Three of the men were from Kigezi diocese. In an act of great personal courage Festo phoned Amin and requested a face-to-face interview. This was arranged and Festo chose his words carefully.

> *Your Excellency, I am troubled about the announcement of the public executions of the men who have been arrested. You have often said that you hear God, and God created human life in His own image, and therefore I plead that these men be given a chance to defend themselves.*

> *You see this little boy of yours, sir? God will give him as long as he needs to grow into a man. So when you think of taking away life, first give it as long as possible before you take it away.*

The best way to relate this sad incident is to let Festo tell you himself. The following quote is from his book *I Love Idi Amin*.

> *February 10 began as a sad day for us in Kabale. People were commanded to come to the stadium and witness the execution by firing squad of the three young men of our area. Death permeated the atmosphere in that stadium. A silent crowd of about three thousand was there to watch the spectacle.*

> *I had permission from the authorities to speak to the men before they died, and two of my fellow ministers were with me. They brought the men in a truck and unloaded them. They were handcuffed and their feet were chained. The firing*

squad stood at attention. As we walked into the centre of the stadium, I was wondering what to say to these men in the few minutes we had before their death. How do you give the Gospel to doomed men who are probably seething with rage?

We approached them from behind, and as they turned around to look at us, what a sight! Their faces were all alight with an unmistakable glow and radiance. Before we could say anything, one of them burst out: 'Bishop, thank you for coming! I wanted to tell you. The day I was arrested, in my prison cell I asked the Lord Jesus to come into my heart. He came in and forgave me all my sins! Heaven is now open, and there is nothing between me and my God! Please tell my wife and children that I am going to be with Jesus. Ask them to accept Him into their lives as I did.'

The second man told us a similar story, excitedly raising his hands, which rattled his handcuffs. Then the youngest said:

'I once knew the Lord, but I went away from Him and got into political confusion. After I was arrested, I came back to the Lord. He has forgiven me and filled me with peace. Please tell my parents (they are evangelists in the diocese) and warn my younger brothers never to go away from the Lord Jesus.'

I felt that what I needed to do was to talk to the soldiers, not to the condemned. So I translated what the men had said into a language the soldiers understood. The military men were standing there with their guns cocked, and bewilderment on their faces. Those in the stadium who were

near enough could hear it too, and the rest could see the
radiance on the faces of the condemned which showed they
were forgiven souls. The soldiers were so dumbfounded at
the faces and words of the men they were about to execute
that they even forgot to put the hoods over their faces!

The three faced the firing squad, standing close together.
They looked toward the people and began to wave,
handcuffs and all. The people waved back. Then shots were
fired, and the three were with Jesus.

For those reading this today it is hard to imagine what a responsibility it was to be a Christian leader in those days and under those circumstances. Even today churches are often persecuted, brutalized and bombed, but then in the 1970s there were no cell phones, digital cameras, internet or Facebook to spread the news quickly. Thus the rest of the Christian community could not share the burden of grief immediately as we can today. There was a sense in which Festo and his leadership, in that moment of time, stood alone, except for the ever-present power and presence of God.

Festo went back to Amin on several occasions to confront him with the enormity of what he was doing. He became a hero to the Kigezi diocese, who spent nights and days in prayer for his safety. On one occasion Festo went so far as to read a protest document from the bishops on television, in which they chided Amin.

In addition to all those pastoral concerns there was still the local work of AEE to consider and there were already

some fairly serious problems in the little team. Michael
Cassidy and Keith Jesson flew to Uganda for meetings with
both the Board and the team to try and help sort matters
out. At Ntebe immigration the authorities sought to keep
Michael out on the grounds that his passport described him
as a 'missionary'. When Michael protested, he was told that
President Amin did not like missionaries. Said Michael to
the immigration official, 'Sir, are you a Christian?' To which
the official replied, 'Yes I am.' 'Then how can you keep
out a fellow Christian?' asked Michael. At this the official
relented. Next day in the Caltex office of businessman John
Wilson, a couple of Ugandan government officials arrived,
probably plain clothes police, and asked if Michael Cassidy
was present. John Wilson replied in the affirmative. They
then instructed that Cassidy and Wilson should follow them
to some government offices. John Wilson was exceedingly
anxious because these were the times in which, as they
said, 'people got disappeared'. Sometimes they were put
in the boots of cars, driven off and never seen again. But
Wilson and Cassidy were at peace as they went back to the
immigration department where the official informed the
men that Cassidy had to leave by the next plane. Michael
politely and boldly declined, saying that he would not be
leaving by the next plane, but only the next plane that went
back to Nairobi and on to Johannesburg. This meant he
would only leave the next day. The key thing was to be in
Kampala for the Board meeting that evening. The authorities,
unaware of the key meeting, agreed that the next day would
be acceptable. The extended Board meeting that night went
on until midnight and the serious issues were sorted out.
These related to whether Festo could continue to lead the
team while also being an ordained Anglican minister. Both

Michael and Keith were in accord that if the Uganda team were to flourish it was essential that Festo be the leader, a view that Festo also held. The matter was amicably resolved. Next day Michael and Keith flew out with a sense of 'mission accomplished'.

Over the previous two or three years John Wilson had been feeling a sense of call out of the business world and into the AE ministry. But Mary, his wife, had been very uncertain, cautious and was holding back. But as Michael was ejected from Uganda, that very same day Mary said to John, 'If Amin can throw out of Uganda people like Michael, then I believe you need to respond to the Lord's call and go into African Enterprise.' This is exactly what happened. So the devil having overplayed his hand in Michael's expulsion from Uganda resulted in John Wilson getting the green light and go ahead to go into the Lord's work. This was a major move and an important appointment for AEE. John was a brilliant man, a totally gracious Christian gentleman, and a person with the spirit and gifting of a senior diplomat. He would later act as Bishop Festo's deputy in AEE.

Bishop Festo himself continued to be involved with AEE and important doors opened through Festo for AE ministries overseas, especially in the Episcopalian and Anglican worlds, but in many other denominations as well. Festo walked through those doors as often as he could.

He continued his many travels abroad, often when others wanted him in Africa. Festo had invitations from all over the world. His many absences from Africa were often a source of frustration to people, especially AEE, who saw doors simply wide open across Africa, let alone other continents. But the message of the East African Revival needed to be heard far and wide, and Bishop Festo was Africa's one great internationalist — the one person with a genuine worldwide ministry. So Cassidy saw that Festo's calling was proper in the greater scheme of things.

By the summer of 1973 Amin had killed an estimated ninety thousand people. Yet despite the turmoil the gospel work continued. The economy was in a shambles. The vast Asian wealth was squandered, machinery remained in disrepair, dairy farms were given to butchers, household goods were hard to find.

Nevertheless the Christians managed to hold the Keswick Convention with Gottfried Osei-Mensah, later himself to join the AE ministry as an International Assistant to Michael Cassidy, as the speaker. In spite of the political climate young people pushed forward to become Christians. Meetings were crowded and the Roman Catholic bishop told his people that when Festo was preaching in the area they should 'go and hear the gospel'. It was at this time that Festo's first book was published, called *When God moves in Revival*.

Amin's terror began to escalate. He announced on radio that there was only one Christian church in Uganda, the Roman Catholics. Then there was a false report of Festo's death in a car accident. The bishops prepared a reply which went into all the papers assuring everybody that he was alive and well — to everybody's relief. Then Festo was off again.

At this point the famous Lausanne Congress of 1974, organized by the Billy Graham organization, was coming up and Festo was to be a speaker, as was Michael. Other AE team members from East and South were also due to be there. It seemed a strategic moment to have AE's first Pan African/International Board meeting in Switzerland just before the Lausanne Congress. As team and Board members from both African regions met at Glion, an extraordinary chemistry developed. The meeting was chaired by the great Archbishop Erica Sabiti of Uganda and his amazing spirit of godly love pervaded the meeting. Malcolm Graham, a South African businessman of great ability, had been invited by Michael to join African Enterprise as its Senior Administrator. He was unsure how to respond. But as he shared a room with John Wilson when they had deep Christian fellowship together and also shared their common background in business, and as Malcolm heard of John's call into ministry, so he too felt that he now had the green light to join African Enterprise. Festo and Michael elaborated their shared vision for the ministry around Africa. Something spiritually special was happening. AE was being truly birthed as a genuinely Pan African ministry.

Then it was on to the Lausanne Congress where Festo's plenary address on the ministry of reconciliation and the gospel demands of love mightily impacted the Congress. Michael led the Congress seminar on university evangelism.

Thereafter Festo's travels accelerated. Back he went to Uganda, then back to Europe, then over to the United States, then back again to Uganda, and so on.

There was some dissatisfaction that he should be doing all this travelling when Uganda needed him, and the AEE staff were also frustrated that he seemed to preach more in the cities of Europe than the cities of Africa. But notwithstanding these sentiments, when he was at home Festo threw himself into his diocese's work with his customary enthusiasm.

The many travels, missions, conferences, meetings and experiences of Festo Kivengere are well documented in the official biography written by Anne Coomes. His impact was considerable and his own stature continued to grow. Another book, called *Love Unlimited,* was released. There is just one important meeting to consider before we return to the threat of Idi Amin.

This was the World Council of Churches Assembly in Nairobi in 1975. Here problems of seeking justice and liberation for the poor brushed up against the caution some evangelicals felt regarding participation in political ideologies. Festo's biographer summed up the tension of that time in these words:

Festo found the lack of stress on Evangelism 'immensely disturbing', but perhaps not surprising, in view of the fact the WCC's theological position on salvation was basically universalist, while the evangelicals believed in the need for personal, individual salvation. He was worried by the suspicion that liberal theology was leading to political liberation becoming synonymous with salvation, which, of course, brought one back to the cross of Christ. Bishop Festo was the main speaker at the mass rally on the Sunday, and as at Lausanne, he again focused on the cross — stressing the need for personal salvation. Individuals had to find Jesus if any peace and harmony were to come to wider society. His message was backed up by leading evangelical churchmen in other sessions and papers and committees.

So in the midst of many different theological currents swirling around at that time, he never lost his focus.

The next chapter moves to the critical moment in Festo's life — his final confrontation with Idi Amin, 'the last king of Scotland'.

10

HIGH NOON

The year was 1977. One hundred years previously, on 30 January 1877, the first CMS missionaries to Uganda arrived and this triggered off a series of events which finally led to the founding of the Church of Uganda. Those early years were marked not only by blessing but also by suffering. There were some notable martyrdoms as the gospel came to Uganda.

That same weekend 100 years later another chain of events was triggered which led to the martyrdom of the Archbishop of Uganda and the exile of Bishop Festo.

The year began with Festo's usual travel abroad, then back to Uganda to greet his first grandchild born to his daughter, Peace, in Kampala. Then on to Kabale where he was to preach at the consecration of Yorum Bamunoba, the first bishop of the newly formed diocese of West Ankole.

It was a great occasion. Both civic and religious representatives made their way by foot, ferry, bicycle, lorry or car. 30,000 people attended. Amongst them were government leaders, army, police chiefs, religious leaders and even carloads of security personal. That day Bishop Festo took as his text, Acts 20:24, 28.

> But I do not account my life of any value nor as precious to myself, if only I may accomplish my course and the ministry which I received from the Lord Jesus, to testify to the Gospel of the grace of God... Take heed to yourselves and to all the flock, in which the Holy Spirit has made you overseers, to care for the church of the Lord which He obtained with His own blood.

Bishop Festo personally challenged the government authorities: 'How are you using your authority? To crush men's faces into the dust?' He went on to condemn the use of force and exploitation of Uganda.

Missionaries squirmed but the Muslim governor got up, walked over to Bishop Festo and deliberately shook his hand in thanks.

Then on 5 February Archbishop Janani Luwum (who had succeeded Archbishop Sabiti) was awakened at 1.30am by three armed men who accused him of harbouring illegal guns. Archbishop Janani replied:

> I was called by God to serve Uganda, Rwanda, Burundi, and Boga-Zaire. There are no arms here. Our house is God's house. We pray for the President. We pray for the security

forces. We preach the Gospel. That is our work, not keeping
arms to overthrow the government.

The raiders searched and left, and another Ugandan bishop, Yona Okoth, was also visited by armed raiders indicating how much the noose was tightening for the leadership of the church.

All the bishops, including Festo, went to Kampala where they resolved to write an outspoken memorandum to the President expressing their grievances.

Addressing Amin as His Excellency Al-Haji, Field Marshal Dr
Idi Amin Dada, VC, DSO, MC, it made clear our view of how
far things had got out of control, and how Ugandan citizens
had 'become insecure, afraid and disturbed'.

The bishops said they were 'deeply disturbed' at the raids that had occurred: 'In the history of our country such an incident in the church has never before occurred.' And they wanted Amin to know of their 'shock and protest.' They reminded Amin of his statements that religious leaders had his 'respect' and that 'to search the Archbishop at gunpoint deep in the night leaves us without words. The gun whose muzzle has been pressed against the Archbishop's stomach, the gun which has been used to search the Bishop of Bukedi's house is a gun which is being pointed at every Christian in the church...' The bishops also objected to the pressure being put on Christians to become Muslim, to the attacks of the uneducated on the educated and a 'brain drain' destroying any progress, and the widespread violence. The bishops were quite specific. 'Too much power has been given to members of

State Research, who arrest and kill at will innocent civilians.' Further, they reproached Amin for making himself 'more and more inaccessible' to the Archbishop, a 'gap' which had brought 'estrangement and alienation' between Amin and all Christians. They complained that Uganda was no longer its own master, but under influence of Palestinians, Sudanese, Somalis and Russians, who had 'not the welfare of this country at their heart.' As for bishops preaching bloodshed, as Amin hàd said in his Christmas Day broadcast, 'We were shocked … we waited … to be called by your Excellency to clarify such a serious situation, but all in vain.'

The bishops stressed: 'We are ready to come to you whenever there are serious matters that concern the Church and the nation, you've only got to call us.' By Wednesday the bishops decided that this time they wanted a personal audience with Amin. They would go together in force. But for this, the eight bishops so far in Kampala were not enough. Cars were hastily dispatched, and by Thursday afternoon, 10 February, fifteen of the Church of Uganda bishops were there (two were out of the country, and one assistant bishop stayed in his diocese).

The memorandum was signed by Archbishop Janani Luwum and an audience was requested.

On Monday 14 February Amin sent for Luwum to come alone to the State House in Entebbe. There Amin accused the Archbishop of plotting with the ousted Obote to overthrow the regime. He cited as evidence that children had found stashes of arms near Luwum's home. These accusations were of course utterly groundless but that did not prevent the allegations being repeated on national radio, and on TV and in the official newspaper — *Voice of Uganda.*

At home again Luwum, after discussion with Festo and the others present, drew up a carefully worded letter refuting Amin's allegations. But before they could do anything with the letter they were summoned to a meeting at the International Conference Centre in Kampala. Apparently Amin wanted to address all government officials, members of the armed forces, ambassadors and religious leaders.

Festo and the others decided Luwum should not go alone. So early in the morning of Wednesday 16 February, the Archbishop of Uganda, Rwanda, Burundi and Boga-Zaire was accompanied by Bishop Festo and Bishop Wani. Four other bishops came in an accompanying car.

Amin on the other hand summoned 1,000 troops, groups of governors, administrators, heads of departments, diplomats and all other religious leaders. There was also on display suitcases full of Chinese automatic weapons, ammunition and hand grenades. It was an atmosphere of hatred. The long drawn-out proceedings took place as a sort of staged trial. A memorandum supposedly written by Obote was read out which suggested how arms could be smuggled into Uganda. One way was by using the help of the Anglican bishops who would send them to the Archbishop in Kampala.

At this point Luwum whispered to Festo: 'They are going to kill me. I am not afraid.' Amin demanded of his audience, 'What shall we do with them?' On cue, the troops replied, 'Kill them, kill them!'

The Vice-President then asked all who wanted them shot in public to raise their hands. Every hand went up. 'Put up your hands if you don't want them shot.' Not one hand went up.

Suddenly the Vice-President backtracked saying they would be given a fair trial in a military tribunal. The crowd was dismissed. It was 2.00pm. They had been there since 9.30am.

But the religious and government leaders, diplomats and senior military officers were told to go to the Conference Centre, where the bishops were taken, as well. They were put in a side room with a security officer guarding them. They could hear applause and shouts in the distance but the minutes ticked by and no one came. They were, to all intents and purposes, prisoners.

Suddenly there came an order of dismissal. The guard said, 'You, Luwum, are wanted in that room by the President. He wants to discuss something.' It was 3.30pm. Festo suggested to Bishop Silvanus Wani, Dean of the Province, that he should accompany the Archbishop to meet the President but was ordered away. Janani then turned and smiled at his bishop. 'I can see the hand of the Lord in this,' he said as he meekly walked away with his captors. That was his farewell comment.

A car load of bishops went back to the Archbishop's house but Festo and Silvanus went back to their car and waited. This is how Festo told the story.

> At ten to five Bishop Wani went to find out what was going on. He was told the Archbishop was still in serious

discussions with the President. He wasn't satisfied and eventually spoke to the Chief of Staff of the Armed Forces who told him he thought the Archbishop was still talking with either the President or the Vice-President in the Nile Hotel [next to the Conference Centre]. We waited for a short while and then went to the soldiers who were guarding the Nile Hotel and asked where the Archbishop was and why he was not coming out. We were told he was still talking with the President. They said we could go home; they would bring him in another car. We said, 'No, we are not interested in another car. His car is sitting there. We came with him, it would be embarrassing to go without him.'

In the end, at about five-thirty, we were ordered by the officers to get away because they didn't like us waiting there. We were dressed in our bishops' cassocks and we were the only ones left. The Archbishop's Mercedes-Benz was the only car there — except for a government car parked just in front of it. We had an argument with the security men and one of the officers came up and said, 'This is an order! Get in your car and go!'

We talked with him and told him how embarrassing it was to go back without our Archbishop. He went away and then two military policemen came with guns and forced us to get into the car and go.

As we sat in the car, Bishop Wani said to them, 'I hope you will bring our Archbishop.' They said, 'Yes sir.'

Reluctantly they joined the other bishops. They were helpless and committed themselves to the Lord in prayer. Mary

Luwum was hysterical and demanded to see her husband. Festo and Silvanus took her and the provincial secretary back to the Nile Hotel where the bishops had gathered early in the day prior to meeting the President. They only got as far as the gates. Security turned them away, their driver almost got shot and so they returned to the Archbishop's house.

At 6.30pm that evening the government radio announced the arrest of the Archbishop and two government ministers who had also fallen out of favour with Amin. The next morning, 17 February, Festo and the other five bishops met at the provincial headquarters to pray and discuss how they could get Luwum released. But at 9 o'clock a women burst in with a copy of the *Voice of Uganda* with banner headlines, 'Archbishop and two ministers die in motor accident'. The story the paper told was bizarre. The prisoners had attacked their driver and in the ensuing struggle the jeep had crashed and overturned somewhere near the Nile Hotel and the Research Centre. There was a photograph of the crashed cars — but it showed vehicles which were known to have crashed two weeks earlier and had been awaiting repairs in a nearby garage.

Festo commented: 'We all knew without a shadow of a doubt that the Archbishop had been shot.'

I went with two other bishops to the hospital to claim the Archbishop's body so that we could prepare for a funeral. When we got there we found most of the nurses and doctors in tears. We tried to see the superintendent of the hospital, but could only speak to his deputy. He was signing

a document, and we noticed his hand was trembling. He had
a security man behind him, and we knew what that meant.
We waited for an hour and were eventually taken to the
mortuary where we were told the bodies were.

But they were not allowed in. A nurse later told them that she had seen the Archbishop's body with two bullet holes in his chest. A Christian soldier later told them he had seen the shooting and the running of the vehicles over the bodies of the three men. The rumours were that they were trying to make Luwum sign a confession, which he would not do. Instead he was praying for his captors.

The Minister of Health said they could have the body after the government investigation. The news became public knowledge and a solemn hush fell on Kampala. Bishop Festo prayed with Margaret Ford, the Archbishop's secretary. 'O loving Father, help us to forgive the men who murdered Janani.'

Friday 18 February dawned. Still they were unable to retrieve the body. By now rumours circulated that Bishop Festo had been murdered too. People met him in the street and wept with relief.

By Saturday 19 Festo received news that he was now at the head of Amin's death list and he decided to return to his own diocese. Several of the associates on the Billy Graham team were able to reach him by phone and assured him of their prayers and concern. When Festo and Mera arrived back home they were immediately in danger.

When we arrived ... Kabale was full of security men. We were told that my house had been watched and checked three times already that day. I knew that if I stepped inside, either I would be under house arrest — as good as executed — or they might wait until after I had preached on Sunday and then arrest me.

Their friends were overjoyed to see them alive and insistently urged them to flee at once. 'One bishop's death this week is enough for us,' they said. Festo and Mera decided to leave. They took nothing with them. They left everything behind — clothes, personal possessions, thousands of sermon notes, books and furniture.

That same night soldiers called on the home of one of Festo's clergyman. They wanted him to say that Festo had brought guns to fight Amin. When he denied this they took him to the Nakasero State Research Prison and tortured him.

Festo and Mera were assisted in the flight by a young couple who drove them into the darkness in a Land Rover. Avoiding roadblocks, and travelling over rough terrain they reached the remote village of Kacerere. This was where the road ran out and Festo and Mera had to flee on foot. Mera was ill with bronchitis and a fever but friendly parishioners guided them. They climbed the mountain track to a height of 9,000 feet and on Sunday 20 February reached the Uganda – Rwanda border.

Festo later told a friend. 'You will never know fear until you are running at night for your life in your own country.'

They were utterly exhausted but sat on a rock over the border in Rwanda and praised God. While they tramped through the Rwandan forest, back in Kampala 4,500 Christians defied government threats and met in the cathedral to remember their Archbishop and to sing the Ugandan martyrs' song.

Meanwhile back in Rwanda, Festo and Mera encountered a Christian businessman with a car — the only vehicle for miles. He gave them a ride to the country's capital Kigali eighty miles away. They knew a pastor there and hours later they were dropped off at his front door. This pastor had heard the news and was praying for the Kivengeres. He went to the front door to see who had arrived. Later, Festo commented that when he saw them, he almost had a heart attack.

11

'I LOVE IDI AMIN'

Festo and Mera eventually made it to Nairobi where they stayed with friends. They were very shaken by their experience and were concerned for those they had left behind. Other bishops joined them in Nairobi as a mass persecution began in Uganda against all those deemed to be in opposition to Amin. Many died, including hundreds of Christians. Their daughter Charity was still in Kampala sitting her final exams. While Mera stayed on in Nairobi to wait for Charity, Festo flew first to Europe and then on to Pasadena in California where the African Enterprise office was located and where generous people provided an apartment for the Kivengeres' use.

Festo was often interviewed in the media in the following months. He was asked difficult questions but was very discreet in the way he replied. When asked why he fled while others had stayed, he replied that he was targeted as a troublemaker because of his blunt way of speaking against the brutality, torture and dehumanization of every kind, occurring in Uganda. Some of his fellow bishops in Kenya criticized him for not making more of a fuss after Archbishop Luwum's death, but Festo was adamant that enough had been said and the ordinary work of caring for the flock had to continue.

Festo also refused to simply condemn Amin. He said, 'I am condemning evil because evil is bigger than Amin... Indeed Amin was a man we loved, we have prayed for him...' (note, *Biog.*, pp. 372, 473).

Festo preached to overflowing congregations and spent a busy period speaking to influential churches and political leaders about Uganda. His daughters, Peace and Charity, were still in Kampala. Charity had already had some unpleasant experiences with the soldiers. Peace was married and had a changed last name which helped, but Charity was taking her finals for her degree at Makerere University and was still exposed to possible harassment. She eventually fled to Nairobi to be with her mother.

Festo eventually grew a beard and changed his mode of dress because the word was out that Amin had armed assassins looking for him. Now African Enterprise (AE) was able to help. After a meeting in London with Festo and other church leaders, AEE established RETURN. The acronym stood for 'Relief, Education, and Training of Ugandan Refugees Now'. In Nairobi AE had been flooded with Ugandan refugees who knew one place where they would receive succour and help would be at the East African headquarters of Festo's work. In the end AE, with Festo as its mouthpiece, raised vast funds for over 300 often prominent Ugandans to study at universities in the Western world. Many would return after graduation and after the Amin era to assume significant places in government and society and they always felt profoundly indebted to the AE ministry. Sometimes Michael Cassidy would also join Festo in bringing the Ugandan story and plight to the wider world.

Festo travelled thousands of miles and preached to thousands of people. His exhausting schedule and the emotional reaction to his own ordeal was beginning to settle on him. His friend had been murdered, his home was in danger of being pillaged, his daughters nearly arrested — all was too much. Although he consistently stated in public that his attitude was one of love and forgiveness, nevertheless a weariness, sadness and discouragement set in. His biographer, Anne Coomes, describes a special spiritual encounter Festo had with God at All Souls Church in London shortly after his flight from Uganda.

> On Good Friday he was alone. He walked up London's teeming Regent Street to the 'BBC church', All Souls, Langham Place (next to Broadcasting House) — an old favourite since his student days in the late 1950s. He quietly slipped in to join the congregation for the three-hour service of meditation upon the crucifixion. It was the first time for weeks that he had had the opportunity of attending a church as a private, individual Christian to worship, to pray and to reflect, rather than to minister. Gradually his thoughts settled themselves. He began to wait on God in prayer.

> The congregation was quietly invited to reflect on the death of Jesus and how it would affect their lives now.

> *The crucifixion story was read out, and the words, 'Father,*
> *forgive them; for they do not know what they are doing'*
>
> (p. 375).

Festo himself tells us what happened in his book
Revolutionary Love:

> *One deep lesson many of us struggled with has been to*
> *forgive the unforgiveable. Many have argued with me about*
> *the title of my little book, I love Idi Amin. And I can only go*
> *back to that first Good Friday after our escape from Uganda.*
> *We were in England and the newspapers were reporting*
> *daily the increased persecution back home. The six young*
> *actors who were to have represented the early martyrs of*
> *Uganda in a play for the church's Centennial Celebration were*
> *found dead together in a field. And on and on. With the pain*
> *we had already gone through, I felt something was strangling*
> *me spiritually. I grew increasingly bitter toward Amin, and*
> *was, to the same degree, losing my liberty and my ministry. I*
> *slipped into the back of All Souls Church in London to listen to*
> *the meditations on the seven last words of Christ on the cross.*
>
> *The first word was read distinctly: 'Father, forgive them; for*
> *they do not know what they are doing.' So said my Lord,*
> *when the cruel nails were being driven into His hands. His*
> *amazing love pressed into my consciousness. To me He was*
> *saying, 'You can't forgive Amin?'*
>
> *'No, Lord.'*
>
> *'Suppose he had been one of those soldiers driving the nails*
> *into my hands. He could have been, you know.'*

'Yes Lord, he could.'

'Do you think I would have prayed, "Father, forgive them, all except that Idi Amin?"'

I shook my head. 'No, Master. Even he would have come within the embrace of Your boundless love.' I bowed, asking forgiveness. And although I frequently had to repent and pray again for forgiveness, I rose that day with a liberated heart and have been able to share Calvary love in freedom. Yes, I have forgiven him, and am still praying for him to escape the terrible spiritual prison he is in

(p. 80).

Two days later, on Easter Sunday, Festo preached his first sermon in Britain since leaving Uganda. It was at Emmanuel Church, Northwood, where his friend Richard Bewes was the rector. Richard Bewes was now also the head of AEE for the UK. Festo passed on his discovery.

Resurrection is not for upright people. It's for broken-hearted people, the defeated and shattered... Before Christ died and rose again, suffering was meaningless, empty, a shattering experience which made life bitter. Then Jesus died in suffering and pain, and he covered suffering with love — victorious, holy love. This kind of love will never be conquered!

It was the secret of what he had found. And it was the same with the Church of Uganda. He read the congregation a letter a friend had sent him from Uganda telling of the outpouring of grace on the people since Archbishop Luwum was killed.

He attended a memorial service at Westminster Abbey. He was the only Ugandan bishop able to attend. Eventually a new Archbishop was elected for Uganda. His name was Silvanus Wani and he was Archbishop of Uganda, Rwanda, Burundi and Boga-Zaire. Festo also received news that original plans to divide his diocese of Kigezi into two, because of the large numbers of Christians and church members, had been put on hold. An 'acting bishop' was installed in his place and his home was occupied with a pastor, his wife and two sons to keep an eye on things. They were threatened and harassed by soldiers wanting news of Festo's whereabouts. They painted the sign 'Property of Kigezi diocese' on all the contents hoping to convince the soldiers that the property was not privately owned.

Festo settled quickly into life in America, and with the help of Dorothy Smoker, a retired missionary with African Enterprise, had published a book called *I Love Idi Amin*. The title was controversial but it became a Christian bestseller and had considerable influence.

Festo's travels now extended to Norway where he preached at large conferences. He also preached at the Cathedral of Trondheim. Then at a news conference later in Germany, Festo was quizzed about the difference in his attitude of love and non-violence, as opposed to the views of theologian Dietrich Bonhoeffer and the Christian group who tried to assassinate Hitler during World War Two. Festo replied to them.

> *I don't want to charge Bonhoeffer and the Christians who were involved in this attempt, but for me and for us*

in Uganda, it is clear: God doesn't need our bullets. If he wants to stop Idi Amin, He can send him a heart attack or something else. Our experience in the past was that after an attempt like that, Idi Amin has killed many persons whom he thought might have been involved. A bullet can kill, but a bullet cannot heal

(*Biog,* p. 380).

Later on he added:

They say that if you use violence — knock out the tyrannical oppressor with a bullet, perhaps — you'll bring about quick change. But the Lord was aiming at a redemptive change, one capable of moulding a new community, a new outlook, a new value of life... The new, revolutionary, way was healing the person.

In one interview Festo was asked what he would do if while present with Idi Amin, the President offered him a gun to fight. Festo replied: 'I would hand it back to President Amin and say, "Sir, this is your weapon. My weapon is love and the Bible."'

Then he was off on his travels again to the USA at the invitation of Billy Graham. He then returned to Norway, where he was one of four winners of the first International Freedom Prize. He was also awarded the Distinguished Public Service Award of Messiah College, Grantham, Pennsylvania.

The year 1978 was bad for Uganda as the killings continued in spite of denials of human rights abuses by Amin. It was also a busy year for Festo. He joined Michael Cassidy for missions in Panama, Egypt, and most notably Australia. This was their first major exposure together to Australia and it led on to AE developing a very strong base of prayer and financial support there, and one of the best offices in the AE ministry. In Australia everybody was all over Festo with excitement because of the Ugandan drama and all its publicity. One person in Australia said to Michael, 'Do you find it hard being second fiddle to Festo in this way?'; to which Michael replied: 'It would be a privilege just to carry his briefcase! And sharing the ministry and the pulpit with him just puts extra cherries on the top of that privilege.' Both Festo and Michael were dynamic in their preaching, with many people responding to the call of the gospel. Here was a black African man preaching alongside a white African man. Both were African evangelists, both had a passion for people to be brought to faith in Christ, both men loved Africa passionately.

Michael tells the following amusing story of how he had dealt with the envy issue once and for all, nearly ten years previously when Festo and he were preaching in the citywide mission to Nairobi in 1969. As the two men preached alternately day after day, a point came when Michael felt some envy in his heart because Festo seemed to secure larger responses to his evangelistic preaching than he did. Michael knew this wasn't good. So one day he asked Festo to come and have coffee with him. 'Festo,' Michael confessed, 'I want to walk in the light with you and share that I have been feeling some envy in my heart because of the much greater responses to your preaching than there are to mine. I feel awful about this. But it is there, and I feel I should confess it.' At this Festo began to laugh. A mystified and slightly distressed Michael said to him, 'What are you laughing at?' Still chuckling, Festo went on: 'You know, Michael, for many years I travelled round the world with William Nagenda sharing about the East African Revival. Wherever we went William was always the centre of attraction, always the better speaker, always secured better results, and always captured the limelight. I was just a second fiddle backup. So one day I went to William and confessed that I had been feeling some jealousy and envy for him.' At this point Festo's face almost crumpled with laughter as he went on: 'You know, Michael, what William's response was? He just began to laugh out loud in a way that almost embarrassed me and made me angry. And he replied: "You know what, Festo? I used to travel many years ago in the early years of revival around the world with Joe Church who was one of the men who God used to initiate revival in East Africa. Wherever we went Joe was the centre of attraction, he was the big shot, everybody poured around him, he was the better speaker, and he always seemed to secure better responses and better results than I. So, Festo, I felt I had to go to Joe and confess this envy." And guess what? Joe began to laugh...!!' And so it went. Festo and Michael now really laughed together as Festo heard Michael's confession and forgave it and the two men were out in the clear and in light and that problem never occurred again in Michael's heart.

Festo's fame increased with each public appearance. Churches, radio stations, TV stations all wanted a piece of him. The ministry of AE was also growing. Many invitations came from outside Africa. Thus a ministry that was commenced with Africa in mind now found itself spilling over into the wider world. In the mission to Cairo word reached the team that Amin's assassins were asking about Festo. After an initial hesitation the mission went ahead with great affect. Crowds thronged the meeting which the team found amazing, for they were in the heart of a Muslim country. Michael and Festo preached at meetings in tandem. Later on in 1978 he attended the Lambeth Conference where he was able to catch up with other Ugandan bishops. Still, caution was needed because Amin had sent along a large 'press corps' to keep an eye on the bishops. Some tension still existed between Festo and some of the other Ugandan bishops but eventually all agreed that Festo would accomplish more for Ugandans while he was in exile than he would if he had stayed in his diocese.

Then to Montreal, then back to Nairobi for a mission with Michael Cassidy where they were greeted very warmly, not only by the churches but also by government officials, amongst whom was Miss Margaret Kenyatta, the late president's sister. After one meeting she told Festo, 'You people must keep preaching to us! You see some of our hearts are so tight closed.'

Festo's schedule was so tight that he had to fly to Holland for a mass youth rally covered on TV, then fly back overnight to preach at the closing rally in Nairobi where both he and Michael preached with hundreds of people responding to the evangelistic message. This meeting was followed by dinner then both Festo and Michael flew to the UK.

Meanwhile as 1979 came round, the world was riveted by news of the war unfolding in Uganda. Amin had tried to divert attention from his suffering country by invading

Tanzania. But the invasion failed and thousands of Amin's troops deserted, leaving a large array of weapons which the Tanzanians commandeered.

President Nyerere of Tanzania in turn invaded Uganda. He took the southern stronghold from Amin's army and paused there, hoping to provoke a popular uprising against Amin. But the people were too cowed to revolt. Yet they left dozens of scribbled notes pinned to trees for the Tanzanian army which simply said, 'Don't leave us.'

Festo and the AEE team began to arrange appeals for relief which was surely going to be needed soon. Nyerere consulted with other Ugandan leaders, including ousted President Obote, and then finally his troops, accompanied by the Ugandan National Liberation Army, marched on Kampala where Amin was making a last desperate stand. Again Nyerere paused. Who would rule after Amin was ousted? Bishop Festo flew to Dar es Salaam to meet with other leaders and exiles to support Yusufu Lule, a former university lecturer, as the new president. Lule was a Christian convert from Islam. Interestingly enough, some even muted the idea of Festo taking over Uganda as its new president. But Festo told Michael a number of times that he had no interest whatsoever or aspirations of any sort to assume political office.

On Monday 9 April Idi Amin fled Kampala, assisted in his escape by Libya. The next day Tanzanian troops took Kampala. Men and women cheered, drums beat, people climbed onto the tanks as they rolled through the ravaged city. The Uganda National Liberation Front took over the country and Yusufu Lule was installed as interim president.

Bishop Festo abandoned his diary even though various churches and organizations had spent a lot of money to organize meetings for him in England. He publicly thanked Nyerere for saving the people from Amin.

Now the biggest and in many ways the most far-reaching phase of his ministry had begun. It would take up the rest of his life. At Lule's invitation Festo became the first Chairman of Uganda's and the Church of Uganda's National Committee on Relief and Rehabilitation. In that capacity he would attract millions of pounds and dollars of aid into the country.

Amidst the calls for reconciliation and all the busyness of organizing relief for the impoverished people, Festo flew to Pasadena to fetch Mera and to help the organization to transport the first shipment of aid to Uganda from AEE, World Vision and other Christian organizations.

A new day had begun.

12

A NEW ERA

Festo Kivengere's return to Kampala was an ecstatic affair. He, Mera and several other Ugandan bishops landed at Entebbe airport. Included in the welcoming committee was Yusufu Lule, the President of Uganda; the Archbishop of Uganda, Rwanda, Burundi and Boga-Zaire, Silvanus Wani; the Roman Catholic Bishop of Kabale, and various members of the AEE team. The media was also present, including representatives from *Time* magazine, *Newswalk* magazine, CBS, a Dutch film crew and an AE film crew who made a film of his homecoming, *Return to Uganda.* Many other friends were present and as they disembarked crowds shouted and wept their welcome. Festo spoke into a large microphone and gave an emotional greeting (*Biog.*, p. 394).

After the airport welcome they moved on to a formal reception at the State House near the airport. He was welcomed by President Lule who warned him that the Uganda he had returned to was not the same as the one he had left. 'There is no respect for life, no respect for individual property ... the type of behaviour we used to know has disappeared' (p. 395). The President stressed the role the churches would need to play in reconstruction and reconciliation.

On their way into Kampala, Festo and Mera stared out of the car windows in horror at the sight of blasted buildings, torn-up streets, people in rags and general shambles. Premises of the State Research Bureau, Amin's dreaded secret police, had been opened to reveal torture chambers and rotting corpses. Generally, in the streets anarchy continued as the liberation soldiers were not disciplined and their drinking and carousing led to more violence and looting.

They went to Namirembe Hill to the cathedral. Thousands of Christians applauded as Festo, Mera and the other bishops entered. The next morning they set out for Kabale accompanied by a large entourage. They stopped to make a tearful reunion with retired Archbishop Erica Sabiti.

Thousands awaited their arrival. Bands played, choirs sang, schoolchildren cheered. Garlands were flung over their necks. It was a very emotional time for them all. Then at the entrance to Kabale 10,000 people were waiting for them.

> It is a great, great joy — I can't put into words — to feel in Uganda the fresh air of liberty, to look around, no guns at one's back ... Jesus Christ using ordinary people like Tanzanians and Ugandans has brought this liberation — I simply have no words except to say, 'Praise God!'

> ... the hope of coming back never died. We waited for the return every evening listening on the radio, I feel absolutely in another world ... it is true we have ... very deep wounds,

deep sufferings, but Uganda is not destroyed. This country is
a country of the resurrection and we are going to come and
tell Ugandans to recover from frustrations, intimidations,
hiding their heads, and say it is a new day!

(p. 398).

Returning to their own home later was yet another emotional experience. They had fled in great fear. Now the home was crowded by friends singing a welcome.

A welcome feast was held at Kigezi High School. Finally Festo and Mera went to sleep, exhausted, but thousands of Christians stayed on and spent the night under the stars around a huge fire in the compound, singing and praying.

The following morning 25,000 turned up at the cathedral service, although only 3,000 could fit inside. Then they went into the amphitheatre where he preached to a vast crowd for two hours, breaking down a number of times. Later he joined the congregation in singing and dancing the afternoon through.

But once the joy and excitement of his homecoming had settled, he had to face the nightmare of what had become of Uganda. His biographer wrote:

There are estimated to be half a million orphans. Some are
starving and many are cold from lack of clothing ... Hospitals
are stripped of medicines ... with very few nurses and
doctors left ... it is reported that Masaka and Mbarara look
like Hiroshima, without a building standing ... farms have
been destroyed, with cattle looted ... in the last eight years

> *not one school has been built, not one hospital, not one*
> *road repaired. Everywhere there are shattered buildings, a*
> *shattered economy ... national credit for urgent purchasing*
> *needs from other countries is non-existent because of the*
> *enormous debts left by Amin.*

Now the UNLA troops were out of control and the new President Lule faced increasing political tensions. Bishop Festo and AEE began work right away. They worked night and day to organize the beginning of the reconstruction of Uganda. Tons of food, medicine, clothes and other relief had been arriving from AE supporters around the world as well as sympathetic western governments and other relief organizations.

A basic relief and reconstruction plan was hammered out. But alongside this, Bishop Festo and the AEE teams launched a programme to tackle the tremendous spiritual needs of the people. They established pastoral seminars up and down the country. He also spent a hectic time in his own diocese visiting churches, people, leaders and clergy. The roads were shocking, the travel was consequently slower, but thousands of people walked miles to see him.

He visited Germany in June 1979 to speak at a vast youth rally but had to rush back to Uganda because of another political crisis. President Lule had been sacked and a British-trained lawyer named Godfrey Binaisa had been installed. But it led to more tensions, with Festo missing out on a trip with Michael Cassidy around South Africa, so that he could join denominational leaders in writing a letter of protest to Binaisa. Binaisa invited Festo to meet him. Festo was to represent all the religious leaders. They talked privately for over three hours.

The country was severely damaged. Malnutrition was rampant. There was no agriculture or transport and the economy was out of control. Festo took his concerns to other African leaders when he preached in their countries, and many attended his evangelistic rallies which were packed out beyond all expectations.

Festo continued to travel internationally but discovered that he had to defend the position he took in his book *I Love Idi Amin*. Some accused him of not understanding their sufferings and loss, and others accused him of condoning the evil. This is always the risk Christians take in matters of forgiveness, especially when the offences have been heinous beyond all belief.

Festo acknowledged how fortunate he was to have suffered so little, comparatively speaking. He argued his case on the grounds of the gospel of grace.

> ...Having been captured by Calvary love, you and I have only one option — the same time that we are hating and protesting against the evil, we love those who oppress us until they are set free from the bondage of oppressing... Violence can never create. In the spirit of forgiveness, people love their enemies until they become brothers. Only those who love like that can change things. Even when they can't change the political situation, they can change the attitude, the destructive disposition which had invaded the community

(p. 341).

In his book *I Love Idi Amin*, written before Amin was ousted, Festo wrote:

> *We look back with great love to our country. We love President Idi Amin. We owe him a debt of love, for he is one of those for whom Christ shed His precious blood. As long as he is still alive, he is still redeemable. Pray for him that in the end he may see a new way of life, rather than the way of death*

(p. 63).

As for Idi Amin, one report stated that he might have suffered from 'hypomania', a form of manic depression which is characterized by emotionally irrational behaviour and emotional outbursts. Whether that is true or not, his brutal regime earned him the title 'The Butcher of Uganda'. Amin fled first to Libya where he stayed for ten years, then relocated to Saudi Arabia. He died in Jeddah on 16 August 2003, outliving Festo Kivengere by fifteen years.

As 1980 dawned, AEE and Festo redoubled their efforts to get relief to the poorest in the country. As he tried to encourage his pastoral team he and Dorothy Smoker, back at the AE offices in the United States, published a book called *Hope for Uganda*. Three years later they published *Revolutionary Love*, detailing his experiences as he retold them in his sermons which Dorothy always had taped, then transcribed, and then edited into books. Festo in one sense never wrote books. He was an eloquent speaker of note and a consummate orator. So the key was to tape everything he said, then after transcribing and editing, get it into book form. Dorothy's services to Festo were monumental. And she gave him a very wide audience amongst Christian readers around the world.

That year also saw the downfall of Binaisa, and Obote eventually regained power. Festo spent his time raising help from his Western contacts and preaching at large AE missions, where hundreds responded to his compassionate appeals. He continued his travels to the USA at the invitation of Billy Graham. He was also able finally to make the trip to South Africa. Michael Cassidy and Festo Kivengere teamed up for an AE ministry tour which took them to Cape Town, Pietermaritzburg, Durban and Soweto. A black and white team at that time in South African history made a huge impact. It was a very significant visit made more so because of the rising tension and anger in South Africa under the apartheid government.

Festo's life was filled with activity, duties in his diocese, travels, missions and relief work, which are all well documented in his official biography. His lifestyle was a cycle of conventions, missions and diocese work. In 1981 he celebrated forty years as a Christian. He summed up his experience.

> *Life is like ploughing a field ... Jesus never came to excuse anyone from pulling the plough of life ... I have a plough to pull in Uganda where I live. You have yours in the place where you are ... you may become weary ... The beauty of Jesus Christ is that He comes and He takes His place by your side... Don't reject your plough. You don't need to change jobs, the problem is not with the plough or the field. You need that special instrument of grace to make the pulling easy ... I don't preach the Gospel because it is my job. In fact, I would be utterly miserable if I refused to preach the Gospel. It is natural for me, the excitement of my life.*

During these years Festo became involved in the controversial
issue of women's ordination. He declared himself in favour
and argued that if modern women kept silent neither the
church nor missions would have achieved what they had
in fact achieved. He proposed the ordaining of women in
Uganda. It was agreed to but it does not seem to have been
practised immediately.

His many travels abroad also brought criticism, some
claiming that he did not earn his diocesan bishop's salary.
His diocese was the smallest but the most successful. Festo
was successful in all he did.

In April 1981 his diocese of Kigezi was split in two. The
first bishop of North Kigezi was to be Dr Yustasi Ruhindi.
A couple of weeks later Festo told his own diocesan synod
of his decision to ordain women. He wrote to all the bishops
and archbishops informing them of his decision which
was warmly supported. There were a number in the wider
Ugandan church who were unhappy but nothing daunted
Festo.

Festo also chaired his last meeting of the Relief and
Rehabilitation Committee. The emphasis was switched
from relief to reconstruction. He continued to travel, but at
home things began to deteriorate and new disillusionment
with Obote set in as the one-time liberator of Uganda from
the violence of Amin became increasingly violent himself
till in the end the deaths under Obote equalled or exceeded
those under Amin. This illustrated one of the principles
articulated in Jacque Ellul's famous book on violence when
he spoke of 'the law of continuity'. The reality is, that once

violence is in the system, it is very difficult to get it out. One of the other Jacque Ellul's laws was 'the law of reciprocity', which means that if you are violent to me I will be violent back to you.

Festo found himself facing new health problems in Uganda: outbreaks of measles, polio and TB. He launched immunization campaigns and drew in Western medical teams to assist. His travels took him back to England and then on to the USA where he appeared on Pat Robertson's Christian Broadcasting Network's *700 Club*, before millions of viewers. Billy Graham welcomed him to his crusade in Houston. Then he returned to Uganda for confirmation tours of his diocese. About 1,350 people were confirmed in two weeks. They spent Christmas in Kabale where 30,000 children were being fed daily by AEE and the immunization programme was gaining momentum.

The year 1982 marked three anniversaries. It was ten years since he had become a bishop; twenty years since Michael Cassidy had first founded Africa Evangelistic Enterprise; and twenty years since Uganda gained independence.

During these times Festo continued with his relief work. His own personal generosity is expressed in a note in his biography that relates how he gave his wife permission to give away his shirts, coats and other clothes whenever she came across 'a brother who had nothing'. This resulted in numerous occasions when he searched his wardrobe for something that was not there anymore. And when he in turn was given gifts of chickens and goats he distributed them in a parish where there was need.

His final years are full of stories of his huge personal ministry, unflagging zeal, indefatigable constitution and the growth of AEE ministries. He and Mera travelled together constantly where she often rescued him from his absent-minded way of losing things.

His travels and his responsibilities both at home and abroad put great pressure on him. But he once said,

> Life without tension is not worth the name ... Christianity survives better in exposure, not when it is protected ... it is those tensions which make life vibrate. You take the tension from the strings of a guitar, and see whether you will get the music...

Amidst all his responsibilities he took up the cause of the Banyarwanda. These were people of Rwandan descent. Uganda had begun expelling them — many of whom had lived in Uganda for generations. But now their property was stolen and their cattle given to others. Festo tried to meet with President Obote and plead their cause. But the president avoided Festo. He was again viewed as a troublemaker; but he never gave up. He sought relief for them. He arranged teams of disaster relief nurses and other helpers for them. Oxfam and UNESCO stepped in to help. He irritated everyone with his pleas for help. He travelled abroad only to return and take up their cause again. Then Mera's brother died. He was the one who, years earlier, had been the young man who gave his testimony which was instrumental in Festo's conversion. At the funeral a young man stood up and confessed to his conversion to Christ and Festo later said,

We burst into a song of praise at the funeral! ... As I looked around, people were clapping and singing and rejoicing ... Is not that continuous revival — when a man who committed himself to the Lord in 1941 dies in 1983 and leads another man to the Lord at his funeral! Praise the Lord His Spirit never dies, He still turns people from darkness to light.

Festo was often frustrated by the events in Uganda, and also at times with the Church of Uganda. It did not always live up to its name. But he told friends:

The work of revival in the church continues not without its ups and downs. But it has never been a smooth run for the Spirit to work in men's hearts. There are always pitfalls and dangers and roadblocks... The church carries with it its tendencies to traditionalism, and tradition is not a very good team member with the Holy Spirit! But we praise God He never allows tradition to take the upper hand. He keeps breaking through...

Festo Kivengere faced many difficult experiences as he continued his worldwide evangelism activities and also carried out his duties as an Anglican bishop in his diocese. In addition he constantly faced up to the political challenges of his day. He maintained that Christians could not be silent in the face of oppression but he also adamantly forbade any of his clergy to be involved in party politics. He continued to challenge Obote in regard to the oppressed Banyarwanda people and expressed his feelings openly and in letters to the President. This was a dangerous way to go but Festo believed in prayer. He explained it like this:

Prayer does not start with you, it is God concerned with His world... He is the one urging you... You will find yourself alongside Jesus in a garden of Gethsemane saying: 'My soul is very sorrowful, even to death', or, 'My heart has been invaded with a kind of sorrow which is about to crush me' (Matthew 26 v 38). It is only when men and women are crushed in love that they can be partners in the redeeming of the world.

Only bleeding hearts can heal bleeding wounds. In prayer you put your hand in the hand of the sufferer, and you share some of his suffering... If you want comfort, you had better be afraid of prayer, because it is going to shock you into the place where the world is. It is going to open your mind, sensitize your personality, and widen your horizons.

Experiencing their suffering, you can whisper a prayer to the throne of grace and that prayer will not be only your prayer, it is the Holy Spirit praying through you for them. He never leaves the desperate to go through it alone.

Festo Kivengere's travels, ministry and relationships were not without controversy. At one stage a split with AEE was only narrowly avoided. On another occasion a new archbishop was needed for Uganda. Festo's name was thrown into the ring but in the event another man was elected. Festo saw this as a sign from the Lord that he should continue with his present ministry and was soon off on his travels again to the consternation of many of his co-workers, both in AEE and in his diocese.

His support for the Banyarwanda people also met with opposition from some who saw his support for them in political terms.

He also went ahead against the misgivings of most of the church in Uganda and ordained three women as deacons to the priesthood. At the service 9,000 people attended and so the issue was overrun by popular support.

Festo Kivengere was probably the most well-known African church leader in his day. Everywhere he went his positive attitude stirred people into action. His stories of the revival, the struggles in the country, the regime of Idi Amin and his spontaneous method of preaching gained him friends and admirers.

On one of his overseas travels he discovered by listening to the radio that Obote had fled the country as immense pressures built up against the tyranny into which he too had fallen. A new man, Yoweri Museveni, became president. Festo wrote out his assessment of Uganda after Obote fled. It was a sweeping analysis which took account not only of the past presidents, but also commented on the factionalism which had developed. He insisted that truth and justice should be the foundation upon which the country should be built.

One December Festo and others visited the slums of Kabale where he had established a parish and a little school. One fellow clergyman, deeply touched, said, 'The harlots and drunks followed him about, wanting to be near him.'

Some of his daughters joined him and Mera for Christmas, but quite unexpectedly he found himself unable to enjoy the reunion. He was not feeling well. He had astounded some of his colleagues of late with little flashes of irritability which were entirely uncharacteristic. He felt unwell and suffered from headaches. Everybody put it down to stress and fatigue. Indeed that would appear the most obvious explanation given his hectic lifestyle. Festo simply ignored the discomfort. Thus he entered into the last two years of his life.

13

FESTO KIVENGERE —
AFRICAN EVANGELIST

Kivengere largely approved of the new president because he believed him to be a good leader who genuinely had the good of the people and of the country at heart. President Museveni's party was the National Resistance Movement, and Festo encouraged his clergy to support it, not for the sake of party politics but because Uganda needed stability and the President needed encouragement from the churches. He wrote: 'As a Christian servant of our land, I am not ashamed to make a contribution to the movement [National Resistance Movement] for a positive change to our wonderful country.'

His words made the news headlines and encouraged other bishops and other denominational leaders to support Museveni. It helped to calm the country because Ugandans had become wary and weary of all governments.

Bishop David Sheppard of Liverpool recalled Festo asking: 'How can the experiences of renewal be turned outwards

in service to the community rather than inward in
sentimentality?' Bishop Sheppard said:

> *It was very important for him that great new experiences*
> *of Christ and His Holy Spirit should turn people outwards*
> *to serve God and people in the life of the world. He was*
> *very concerned at the amount of corruption in public life*
> *in Uganda. He told me that eighty per cent of the people*
> *of Uganda belong to the Anglican and Roman Catholic*
> *Churches, and was disappointed that so few took their faith*
> *into the places where decisions are made.*

Festo wanted more friendship and co-operation between
the Roman Catholics and the other churches to bring
down the climate of hostility — a lot of which was political.
Nevertheless, in spite of what was perceived as an improving
political climate, his good friend and Deputy Team Leader
of AEE, John Wilson, was assassinated in the run-up to
AEE's greater Kampala Mission in which John was the chief
set-up person and director. Festo himself had been delayed
in England with deteriorating health and had been unable
at that moment to get back for the Kampala Mission. What
happened was dreadful. John and his wife Mary were driving
one night through Kampala when they were stopped by a
couple of masked men. These men proceeded to drag John
from the car and shoot him in front of his wife and father-
in-law.

John's daughter Victoria, with whom he had a very close
father/daughter relationship, believes that John was
martyred because of his Christian witness, his prominent
stand against violence and oppression, and his work in
setting up the Kampala Mission. There are others probably

who might say it was just random violence. In any event, whichever way it was, it was a tragedy of note and a desperate blow for Festo. He was very moved when he heard from Mary how John said, 'I feel my life is ebbing away.' And then he prayed: 'Lord, please look after my beloved wife and family as you now take me to Yourself.'

At the funeral both Michael Cassidy and Festo preached. Michael paid tribute to John as one of the greatest African Christian friends that had ever been his privilege to know and one of the finest Christian leaders on the continent. Festo's message was full of the eternal hope that Christians have. He said, 'Heaven — I am longing to join him there. One of these days through sickness or in a car, I will cross over and shake his hand. Of course they don't greet us in Heaven, but never mind, they praise God.'

His longing to join John was close to fulfilment. His headaches, general malaise and irritability continued. He saw a doctor in the USA who gave him a clean bill of health. But arriving back in Nairobi he stumbled and almost fell down the stairs. They saw a doctor in Nairobi who ordered a brain scan, this time in London. He was now experiencing numbness in his leg and arm and the feeling of paralysis was spreading.

He was finally operated on for a tumour at the base of his brain. His whole diocese was praying for him and the operation was a success; but he did not make the recovery that was anticipated.

Festo appeared to be in the advanced stages of Parkinson's disease, but when the balance between the medicines was achieved he made rapid progress. By the end of July of that year (1986) he was able to return to Kabale and to attend the Kabale Golden Jubilee Convention, although he did not preach. For ten days thousands attended the convention and sang revival hymns while Festo stayed at home resting quietly. He managed to attend the closing meeting of the convention when 20,000 attended. While recuperating in Nairobi he again put pen to paper to object to a visit to Uganda by Colonel Gaddafi of Libya. Gaddafi tried to stir up the Muslim community against the Church of Uganda.

In a press release Festo wrote:

If we dwell on digging up the bones of bad things in history the possibility of living in this world together will be nil. We in Uganda had our religious wars in the last century, we do not want any more of those wars here. Moslems and Christians in Uganda, having learnt their lesson, now live together in peace.

I see Moslems in my church listening to the message of God's love. And when I am asked by Moslems to address them I do not hesitate to do so ... This does not mean that I want them all converted when I speak to them; but when they are convinced that it is God's message and they convert, they are free to use their choice without pressure. For instance, if a Christian becomes a Muslim we respect his decision and we do not follow him to kill him, for to us Christians killing a person because of his convictions is completely opposite to our faith. In fact any killing for us Christians is a curse and we do not believe in it

(*Biog.*, p. 450).

Festo surprisingly made rapid strides. So much so that he was able to rescue his preaching engagements. He was off to America, then Norway. Later that year the doctors gave him a clean bill of health. But he wasn't the same. Now sixty-six years old he was showing his age. He decided to retire as diocesan bishop and gave himself fully to the work of AEE. But his diocese would not hear of it so Festo did not set a date. His diary rapidly filled for 1987 and Festo went to Amsterdam for a convention where he preached a sermon on liberation theology. Although his background was revivalist he showed a lot of sympathy for the cause of the liberation theologians. Here is a sample of his take on liberation theologies:

> *Liberation Theology was born out of frustration and disappointment in the established church. The Bible and the traditional liturgy were eulogized. They gave comfort to the members and sweetly sent them to sleep. The radical challenges of the Old Testament prophets on practical injustices, social discriminations, political oppression, economic exploitations and many other evils have been ignored. These evils have spread like cancer without any challenge from the leaders. The church has increasingly become a party in all this, directly or indirectly. Opportunism in politics and social benefits strangled the protesting and rebuking voice. The suffering masses had none to highlight their cause — they became more and more dehumanized and sank deeper into their silent misery. This was the case in Latin America, predominantly (Catholic countries), and in the big cities of Western Europe and the USA. But the same situation does exist in our Third World situations. He had compassion on the harassed and helpless crowd. How*

often the Lord had compassion on the sick, the hungry, the weeping and the like! (Matt 15:32). For me the heart of spiritual liberation is Jesus and Him crucified, risen and reigning among His people. But spiritual liberation never takes place in a spirit without the rest of what makes you and me human. It embraces the whole of me — my rights, dignity, property, security and freedom. Mere political and social liberation do not go far enough. They need a greater dynamic to achieve a whole liberation for the whole person — spirit, body and soul. So the preaching of Christ, the healing and feeding of the body for which He died, and the enlightening of the mind, work in harmony to make man whole in Christ Jesus.

Back home in Kabale, Festo had to take a stand against a new development — that of kidnapping because of political differences. Furthermore he also chose a man from an obscure tribe to serve as the deacon of his cathedral. He stood totally against what he considered ungodly ambition amongst the clergy. In a sermon he had made the following comments:

The mission of His (Christ's) entire life on earth may be summed up in one expression: 'He came to serve in love.' When James and John desired high positions in the ministry — as a means to serve better, to exert more influence, to carry more weight, and exercise more authority they approached Him through their mother to make their request less obvious. But the Lord Jesus saw through the folly of their mistaken understanding of what gives influence to service. It is not the position of the one who serves, not the rank, but the heart flooded with the love of God, in Christ, by the Holy Spirit (Romans 5:5).

So he ministered tirelessly on — inevitable politics, struggling in the streets, endless visitors, confirmations, sorting out troubles in the school and of course, a never-ending stream of missions. He added China to his itinerary and travelled there with a sizeable AE team, where their ministry was wonderfully blessed. Unfortunately, Michael's schedule in South Africa did not allow him to join this Chinese missionary adventure. Festo was able to attend the twenty-fifth anniversary of independence for Uganda but there was not widespread enthusiasm for independence even though President Museveni was working hard to establish order in the country.

Then, shortly after a mission at Makerere University, Festo developed a fever. He was sent to bed in the belief that he had contracted malaria. Other symptoms manifested themselves and finally through the Missionary Flying Doctor services, he and Mera were flown to Nairobi. The Nairobi physician established a bone-marrow abnormality. He was sent to London amidst calls for prayer and then he returned to Nairobi.

In early February 1988 the AE/AEE team was meeting for its annual international conference in a little hotel called Livingstonia on the edge of Lake Malawi. Michael's journal for 5 February runs as follows:

Today the dreadful and shattering news came in a telex from Festo that the doctors say he has four weeks to live. We have been left rocked and stunned and mystified. First John Wilson, and now Festo. Oh, we hold only on to You. Tomorrow before we make the formal announcement to the team, I am doing the Team Leader's report and my theme is going to be 'Great is Thy Faithfulness'. In dark times one has no refuge but flight to that greatest of truths. I spoke to Festo via a very poor phone line tonight. He said that Gresford Chitembo of our Tanzanian team had prayed for his healing. 'I am in good hands, Michael,' he said.

Concludes Michael's journal entry:

Lord we know it. And reaffirm it for Festo. And for all of us. I am weary.

Festo wrote to all the AEE Board Chairmen in USA, UK, Australia, Canada and West Germany, and indeed to the whole AE partnership. He wrote:

All these things, as one Bible writer said, are beyond me, but they are not beyond my Lord. He still is in control and we must hand over the circumstances to the Master. He knows what He is doing. He has never made a mistake. What we do not see today, we shall see tomorrow. All that we pray is that the Lord will save us from panic and keep us under the control of His victorious love.

Since I was informed that mine is an incurable illness — unless the Lord Himself reverses all that, and He can — I have been thinking about our AEE family and the future ministry. We are not shaken backwards; we are shaken forward. These kinds of experiences in the power of the Holy Spirit are springboards from which to jump forward, not deterrents to stop us from moving...

God puts His servants aside and then chooses His servants to take their places. This is normal and we must accept it...

He was treated with chemotherapy. People prayed for him and Michael Cassidy flew up from South Africa to have fellowship with him and be with him for the last time. On 10 March 1988 the two men, deep friends, and partners for many years in the gospel met for the last time in the Nairobi Hospital. Michael's journal records their final sharing and the substance of their conversation.

Festo was in his pyjamas and dressing gown and Mera was there too. Festo unfolded his story in these terms: 'Michael, my brother, prayer has made me ready for Heaven. I can have good news one minute and then bad news the next. I am ready for either. I remember Philippians 1:21 that "For me to live is Christ, and to die is gain." I preached on that at the grave of William Nagenda.

'When I came back from London to Uganda, I was met by many people at the airports, first at Ntebe and then Kigali and they all said they had been praying much for me, sometimes throughout the night. I came back from London not with the assurance that I was going to be healed, but with the assurance that God is able, should He choose to heal me.

'In London a doctor who was a Jew said to me: "Sir, you are a man of God. Sir, I am going to tell you the truth. You have cancer of the blood. And we have no cure for you. I don't want to shock you, but I am afraid I must." Well, I replied to the doctor saying: "Doctor, you are not shocking me. You are only shocking me home to Heaven!" The doctor replied: "I am not God. Our times are in His hands."'

Festo went on as Michael listened, very attentive and very moved:

> 'Michael, I am just feeling a kind of assurance that all is well. But even feeling that, should I shock you, or just put it in nice spiritual language? I have decided to give the news about my condition just as God has given it. I have been blessed that Archbishops and Bishops of Cape Town, Kenya and Uganda, plus others in South Africa from different backgrounds, have written to me to encourage me. Talk about ecumenism, Michael! I tell them, "You are looking at a Lazarus." But Mera has told the kids: "Dad will soon go to Heaven. There is nothing I as your Mummy or others can do about it except pray. So we must do that."'

Festo also shared with Michael that he took hope and comfort from 2 Kings 20 where Hezekiah is first of all told that he will die. 'But as he prays with earnestness and weeping, the word of the Lord came to him saying, "I have heard your prayers and seen your tears and behold I will add 15 years to your life." The Lord can do this for us, Michael.'

At this point Mera chipped in saying, 'Michael, I had to repent. I knew that Festo was ready to die in front of me, but I must not doubt that we are in the Lord's hands.' Then she added: 'I have been blessed by Psalm 100:3 which says: "Know that the Lord is God! It is He that made us and we are His; we are His people and the sheep of His pasture." Michael, we must never forget that the Lord is God.' Michael still has Psalm 100:3 noted in the margin of his Bible with the words '"Never forget that the Lord is God" (Mera Kivengere — Nairobi. 10.3.88 with Festo).'

At this point Mera decided she would leave the room to leave Festo and Michael together. As she left she again repeated: 'I have repented of not having faith in the Lord. All I know is that if Festo dies, I will follow him.' When the two men were alone Festo went on: 'Michael, my brother, I have been getting messages since last November that Heaven was present. All the family were with us for Christmas for the very first time. At the end of November there was pain in my leg and I didn't see the doctors but completed my preaching programme. But then from December 16th to 19th last year I knew nothing. I was in a coma and taken to hospital. My blood count was right down and the doctor said that he couldn't move me or I would have died there and then. Then later I got taken to London to be in hospital there. But I was surrounded all the time by prayer. Oh, it was sweetness! And great blessing came in the way God gave peace to Mera and put the spirit of prayer upon our kids.'

He then reflected on the funeral of his late AE colleague, James Katarikawe, and told how his funeral was like a convention. 'But I did find myself saying: "Lord, what are you doing? Especially taking gems like James away." But I know that the Lord knows what He is doing.'

Festo then discussed all sorts of situations in the AE ministry, needs and personnel in the AE ministry in East Africa, including saying that Bishop Gresford Chitemo of Tanzania was the right one to succeed him in the AEE leadership because he is 'a brother being greatly used'. Festo went on to say that as far as the Uganda team was concerned it was failing to adequately challenge the country, even though the country was open. He then spoke about a younger and upcoming leader for the AE ministry in Uganda in the person of a young man called Edward Muhima. Said Festo,

> *He can lead our team well in evangelism. I knew him as a boy, ordained him as a deacon, priested him, and made him a youth leader. I also got a scholarship for him from the Billy Graham Association to go to Trinity Evangelical Seminary to get his MTh and then North Western Seminary to do his PhD. This young man has told me that he has a call on his life for evangelism. We must encourage the leadership and gifting in our team, but not bring others who are not gifted.*

Added Festo:

> *We have also prayed much for your country, Michael, more in fact than ever before. We have been so blessed by Psalm 100:3 telling us not to forget that the Lord is God, reminding us that we are His, and we are the sheep of His pasture. So I find myself being torn between earth and Heaven even when I can't make sense of my experience. But, Michael, do you remember the story in Exodus 15 when Moses and the children came to Mara (v. 23) and found 'they could not drink the water of Mara because it was bitter; therefore it was named Mara.' Then after the people had murmured to Moses, 'the Lord showed him a tree, and he threw it into the water, and the water became sweet.' You see it there in verse 25. Well my brother, my waters have been bitter, but the Lord has thrown into them the tree of Calvary and now these waters have become sweet.*

Festo then talked a bit more about the AE/AEE ministry and said that, 'if ever competition comes into our ranks, then we have lost Him. We have to remember that the AEE work does not depend on us but on our acknowledged weaknesses. But certainly the team must never be diverted from the essence of reconciliation and we must never be in the place where we do not have the power of the Lord to bring reconciliation. This means restoring the vision of Calvary.'

Michael was then astonished to hear Festo say that he had been reading a book on the cross by Professor Leon Morris, an Australian theologian. Here was Festo, almost on his deathbed, but still reading solid theological material, but not surprisingly that which focuses on the cross.

Festo stressed that it is the Lord that controls all the circumstances in our ministry and Jesus is the Master who never feels mastered.

> That's why we must pray and not stop praying. And the amazing thing is that we can come to the place where there is a lack of striving. And we know that the future of AEE is in the Lord's hands. In fact, He is bringing the whole team much closer to each other. So we must keep looking forward with our assurance placed in Him until we meet at the gates of splendour. And we must keep loving each other. Then the world will see what we are really on about.

Michael was overwhelmed by this time, and especially as the men prayed together for the last time, embraced and kissed each other.

Mera moved into the hospital but to everyone's surprise he began to improve. He gained in strength and looked forward to greater ministry. Eventually there was no trace of the leukaemia.

He formally resigned from the Kigezi diocese. Again he steadily increased in strength and was considering a mission in Birmingham, England, when suddenly he collapsed and was rushed into intensive care. Again he was treated with chemotherapy and again the leukaemia seemed to disappear. It was decided he could go home to his flat in Nairobi. His suitcase was packed when he collapsed again. This time he lapsed into a coma. The greatest evangelist Africa had ever known died that afternoon at 5.00pm. The date was 17 May 1988. The Christian world went into mourning.

A memorial service was held on Tuesday 24 May in All Saints' Cathedral in Nairobi. All AE leaders from around the world and from around Africa gathered there. Thousands came to the cathedral to view the body. The AE leaders then chartered a special plane, which also carried the body, as well as almost every major leader in the AE ministry to fly up to Ntebe, Uganda. One generous overseas Swiss donor later said to Michael, 'I have decided not to give money to you people again because you were so irresponsible and unprofessional as to have all of your leaders fly in one single chartered plane. Just image if you had crashed! That would have been the end of AE!' 'I think this Swiss brother stuck to his vow,' sadly lamented Michael later.

A State funeral on 26 May 1988 was now provided for Festo at the Namirembe Cathedral in Kampala. The President provided a motorcade. The journey was full of clapping, singing and praising God by Ugandan Christians. The memorial service was four hours long to accommodate all the tributes and Michael Cassidy was the preacher. Michael opened his message saying,

> When I heard last week that Festo had gone to be with the Lord, I left my house, which by the way is called Namirembe, so that I can't forget all of you, and I went out into the night and wept. I felt shocked, shaken and at peace all at the same time. I also felt sadness at the loss of a great friend and colleague, but also joy that he was with his Lord whom he loved so much. I also felt deep gratitude to have known him as such a wonderful friend, brother and co-leader of our AE/AEE work for twenty years. Yet I felt also remorse and grief that I had not been to him a better friend, brother and co-leader. The next morning I went into the forest near my Namirembe with a tape of greetings that he had made me and I played it over and over again and wept some more. As always Festo was celebrating Jesus, and his love for Jesus, and constantly saying, 'Isn't He great!'

Michael gave as his text Hebrews 11:4 about Abel 'who offered the blood sacrifice which pleased God'.

> Festo supremely, more than any other major evangelist in the world, preached that greater blood sacrifice of Jesus. But then the text says of Abel that 'he died but through his faith he is still speaking'. Thus it is with Festo, this great man of faith, in whom everything sprang from faith. Yes, Festo has died, but through his faith he is still speaking. Through his life and example he is still speaking. Through his preaching and teaching he is still speaking. Through his family and friends he is still speaking. Through his church

*and diocese he is still speaking. Through his colleagues in the
AE teams he is still speaking. Through his books and tapes
he is still speaking, through his converts and disciples he is
still speaking. And through his memorial services and this
funeral he is still speaking. In fact, such has been Festo's
life and ministry that till Jesus comes again he will still be
speaking, rebuking, evangelising, and inspiring.*

Michael then shared some of their experiences together
across the years and these were a great blessing and
inspiration to the enormous and jammed packed crowd
in Namirembe Cathedral, with hundreds outside in the
courtyard who could not get in.

Mera remarked at the funeral: 'I found Festo's spirit full of
praise just before he died. And the Lord also spoke to me
and said: "Don't worry Mera, I will be with you."'

On 27 May his body was moved to Kabale. Thousands of
Christians waited for the return of the bishop. A thirty-car
escort accompanied them and there was no room to spare,
even in the hotels. Many stayed up all night singing hymns
and praising God.

Throughout the Saturday 20,000 people met in service after
service. The entire cabinet of the Ugandan Government
attended. The cathedral remained open all Saturday night
for singing and praying. President Yosemi Museveni and his
wife arrived by helicopter and the President gave a moving
tribute, which indicated his respect for Festo Kivengere.
Finally at 5.00pm his body was laid in a grave in the grounds
of St Peter's Cathedral, Kabale. While hundreds wept, the

National Police Band played the 'Last Post' and in this way the African church bade farewell to their beloved evangelist.

AEE released the following statement the next day:

> *Bishop Festo ... has been promoted to glory. He has kept the faith, finished the course, and inherited the crown. He has lifted up the name of Jesus. Physically we hurt, but spiritually we rejoice. We know that Festo has gone home.*

Twenty years before, in Switzerland, Festo had said, 'If you should you forget all my words, but you still keep your attention fixed and centred on Jesus, then I will know that my work has been done.'

He did the work of a faithful evangelist. After Bishop Festo's death memorial services were held in Langham Place and the first Bishop of Kigezi, Bishop Dick Lyth, said:

> *His great testimony was the grace of God daily reaching out to a weak and undeserving sinful man; and whenever this testimony of his was diluted, the Calvary love and forgiveness of God was proportionately reduced. And Festo would have none of it*
>
> (*Biog.,* p. 468).

Michael Cassidy recorded in his journal on 28 May 1988:

> *Festo has gone. It is very hard to believe. Or accept. It is even harder to think of a world without Festo, an Africa without Festo, a church without Festo, and especially an AE without Festo.*

He was to be sure a most remarkable man. Not without faults, like all of us. But a prince and a giant nevertheless. And to have preached in Namirembe Cathedral on the occasion of his state funeral has been and will always be one of the greatest privileges and honours of my life. I was not totally happy with my utterance, but most seemed pleased. God is merciful.

What struck me in the funeral was the range of lives and the number of them that Festo had touched. Truly Lord, You used your servant most wonderfully and his tireless proclamation of Your Word and his genius in preaching were beautiful and potent instruments in Your hands.

Of course, Calvary was at the heart of all his utterances and he worked hard to keep his spirit sweet. There was humility there too — though not untinged with the spirit of the kings in the land and region from which he came.

My gratitude to have known him and loved him and be ranged with me in ministry for nearly twenty years, knows no bounds. It has been one of life's special privileges. Thank You, dear Lord.

It is also true that in many ways I regret not having been closer to Festo, and a better friend, colleague and co-leader of AE. Miscellaneous fates worked against this. I think the devil did too. And of course we should have done much, much more together. But politics, both external and internal in those very tough years, did much to impede.

EPILOGUE

What are we to make of Festo Kivengere? His story is all the more interesting and complicated because it is intertwined with the story of revival, a phenomenon not as much understood or appreciated today as it was in the past. Festo's story points us to something unusual that happened in East Africa beginning in the early 1930s and continuing intermittently at least until his death and some claim even up to today. But was it a real visitation of God's Spirit?

The Ugandan Church story referred to in this book is full of great events, large crowds, encouraging conversions but also serious backsliding with church splits and very unseemly behaviour by some. Furthermore these things all occurred during times of great political upheaval in Uganda and the church seemed largely unable to restrain the evil practices of successive presidents and their leaders. So was it all real?

My first comment is to refer to the observations of the one great figure in church history who must rank amongst the most knowledgeable of all analysts of revival — Jonathan Edwards. The biography written by Iain Murray is particularly helpful. In the revival that was poured out in Northampton in 1740, which Edwards witnessed, he identifies elements which he called 'wild fire' with misguided and enthusiastic young Christians. Edwards saw the hand of the devil in the excesses that were experienced. He further noted the problem of new converts who failed, with no fruit being produced by their conversions.

He offered two explanations for this. The first was that a distinction had to be made between the operations of the Spirit of God which are saving and that which were only common. By this he meant that God's power through the gospel sometimes brought a sobering influence to some. It arrested people in their activities and convicted them so that it may appear as repentance and faith. But these experiences do not always lead to saving renewal in the soul.

He asserted in the second place that as the Holy Spirit had been active in producing real converts, so Satan was also powerfully active in producing counterfeit religion. It appeared evangelical, the people seemed to 'experience Christ', and seemed to be affectionately united with him. But they were all counterfeit. Edwards argued that the devil does not seek to counterfeit valueless things. 'There are many false diamonds and rubies, but who goes about to counterfeit common stones?' (*Edwards*, p. 255).

Edwards went on to list the things that are missing from those whose conversion is false and Murray helpfully sets them out for us.

- *True humility is missing.* True Christians are self-effacing and always view others more spiritually advanced than themselves.
- *An abiding sense of sin is missing.* There is no brokenheartedness amongst them. Compare this with the emphasis on brokenness in the East African Revival. But for the counterfeit there is no mourning for sin.
- *A true balance is missing.* A true Christian has both boldness and modesty. He has great confidence yet a soft heart. He is poor in spirit but constantly hungry for God.
- Edwards also insisted that *the love and pursuit of holiness is the enduring mark* of the true Christian.

Thus it seems that revivals throughout history always had difficulties with some people whose behaviour stood out in stark contrast to the blessing of the presence of the Holy Spirit — even though many people started out with what appeared to be genuine conversion experiences.

It should also be borne in mind that a revival is not necessarily a reformation in the sixteenth-century sense of the word. God's Spirit works in different ways in different eras in church history. Some places seem more open and spontaneous in their response to the gospel than others. Even now, as one living in Africa, I can attest that it is relatively easy to speak of Christ in Africa in spite of the onslaught of Western secularism. Thus while Africa is still beset with many problems there is, at least in Sub-Saharan Africa, a great general awareness of the basics of the Christian message. Reformation may bring about sweeping social changes, but revival, at least as it was experienced and understood in East Africa, brought about a great acceptance of the message of the gospel, strengthened churches and has given rise to large populations who, though they may yet be in need of reformation, nevertheless have great sympathy for the church's message of salvation.

Thus revival in some ways seems to be paradoxical. It cuts wide swathes, pulls in huge harvests, influences great numbers of society and creates a general consciousness of the gospel. But it does not necessarily stop all displays of ungodliness in society, nor does it prevent a crisis like the Idi Amin saga, or for that matter the horror of the genocide in Rwanda. Instead, amazingly, when it is all over, there are still churches there with thousands of true believers in Jesus.

Edwards also helps us to remember the reality of Satan. His deception, power and influence are everywhere. When a previous Archbishop of Rwanda, Emmanuel Kolini, visited Cape Town, he said in a meeting I attended, 'People often ask us why the Rwandan massacres occurred in a country that had seen so much revival. How was it possible? I often say to them you do not need to do a theses for a PhD to find out why. I'll tell you. I believe in the devil!' I do not think that Archbishop Kolini meant to imply that all evil things that happen can be blamed 'willy-nilly' on the devil. We know that as fallen people we often make choices that might have severe consequences and so we become our own worst enemies.

Furthermore we must remember that many of the so-called Christians involved in the Rwanda event were not properly taught or discipled. Bible teaching has been sadly lacking in areas where great numbers of people have professed faith in Christ.

But what Kolini referred to, I believe, is the scale of the slaughter in Rwanda, and the hysteria that gripped the nation had its roots in the kingdom of darkness. It was ultimately such an overwhelming event that it could not only be explained in terms of man's sinfulness but also had to be seen in terms of the powers of darkness that appeared to be engulfing this land. Many in Africa would identify with this explanation — a sobering and timely reminder for us all of the power of the forces of evil and conversely the power of the message of the cross to rescue sinners.

Kivengere was a man of his age. Neither he nor the churches around him were perfect. But they had experienced God in an unusual way. I do not think his theology would meet the robust requirements of today. He was a child of the Keswick movement — Christ-centred, pietistic, devotional. His preaching was anecdotal and winsome. It might not fit in easily with much of the evangelical scene as it is today. Our day may demand more accurate theological thinking, although we cannot deny that Festo did indeed read deeply, extensively and constantly in very solid theological material. Yet for all that, Festo Kivengere has a great deal to teach us about personal love for Christ, unflagging belief in the power of the cross to save people and great endurance to the end.

It ought also to be mentioned that Festo was an Anglican, caught up in a great revival movement. He did not have the privilege of being exposed to the good doctrinal heritage of the great Anglican reformers or other good reformed theologians. All he had was what was passed on to him. Many people will bless God for what Keswick has meant to them over the years. This strong pietistic evangelicalism is where Festo stood. Had he had the privilege of exposure to the doctrinal verities of the Reformation, who knows how that may have affected his work, especially the work of discipling the new converts. Yet we must not conclude that Festo was totally unaware of these things. His relationship with John Stott and other evangelical Anglicans did not leave him untouched by these wider and deeper doctrinal views.

Even so, his grip of the doctrine of the cross and the importance of the atonement was a compulsion within him. His whole life was Christ-centred. He withstood storms that may have swept others away because in spite of the lack of formal training he was nevertheless able to face the troubles of his day because of his love for Christ and Christ's hold on him.

It should also be borne in mind that part of the dynamics of his age was the strong presence of both the Roman Catholic Church and of Islam. Festo had to walk very carefully. Emotions could easily be raised and lead to serious consequences. Thus he did all he could to maintain peace between these groups. This should not be read as compromise. It is never easy to be a leader. Various judgement calls had to be made and unless we ourselves have lived under the tensions and stresses the Ugandan Church had to endure we should withhold judgement.

It should further be noted that the story of Festo Kivengere cannot be told apart from his relationship with both Billy Graham and, more importantly, Michael Cassidy. Both men had a huge influence upon him. One of the great calls of the age in which they ministered was that of reconciliation — both politically and also in terms denominational church fellowship. For some, all this activity may have been seen as compromising certain beliefs and doctrines. But, as mentioned above, living in Africa with its tensions, fractured society and volatility took courage and wisdom so that doors would be kept open to preach the gospel.

As to his labours across the world with Michael Cassidy and in the African Enterprise ministry, Festo was very courageously in advance of his times in being willing to demonstrate the spirit and outworking of the ministry of reconciliation by travelling with a white South African colleague and friend at a time when racial tensions were far from settled in Africa. At times working in this way was very testing and exacting, both for Festo and Michael. In the early 80s when tensions and difficulties were very high, Michael shared these words with Dr Tom Houston, then International Director of World Vision: 'It's very hard keeping this whole thing together.' 'But,' Tom responded, 'you and Festo must hang in together. You are, after all, a unique partnership and ministry in the world.'

Thus in Festo Kivengere we have a true African gospel hero. It is true he would not fit neatly into our reformed doctrinal categories. He is not to be understood in that way, rather he is to be seen for what he was, an African, converted in a revival, an Anglican, an evangelical, a pastor to his people, a thorn in the side of evil leaders, a man who brought hope to his people with the preaching of Christ crucified and risen.

Festo did not lead a reformation. God knows how much Africa needs that. Rather he led a revival through which thousands became believers. But Kivengere and his contemporaries, whether in the church of Uganda, or in African Enterprise, were gripped with Christ and his cross. Festo understood the cross sufficiently enough to know it was our only hope and presented it as such. Kivengere was Christ's man, and Christ was Kivengere's Saviour and Master.

We cannot emulate his great gifts, enormous confidence or oratorical style — nor should we do so. But all he had, he gave to the task of evangelism and renewal. In that role he stands as a continuing example to us. May God raise up many men and women in Africa, this great continent, so full of restlessness, potential, sadness and exuberant joy, to be like Festo Kivengere — an African evangelist!

FURTHER READING

The Authorized Biography of Festo Kivengere
Anne Coomes, published by Monarch, 1990

This is essential reading for anyone who is interested either in the subject of the biography or the effects and phenomena of the East African Revival.

African Harvest
Anne Coomes, Monarch UK, 2002

A God-Sized Vision
Collin Hansen and John Woodbridge, Zondervan, 2010

Evangelical Awakenings in Africa
Edwin Orr, Bethany Fellowship Inc., 1975

Revolutionary Love
Festo Kivengere with Dorothy Smoker, Christian Literature Crusade and Kingsway Publication, 1983

I Love Idi Amin
Bishop Festo Kivengere with Dorothy Smoker, Marshall, Morgan and Scott, 1977

Love Unlimited
Bishop Festo Kivengere with Dorothy Smoker, Regal Books, 1975

Jonathan Edwards — A New Biography
Iain H. Murray, The Banner of Truth Trust, 1987

The Religious Affections
Jonathan Edwards, Volume III, Banner of Truth Trust, 1961

Festo Kivengere
Dictionary of African Christian Biography — Frederick Quinn
http://www.dacb.org/stories/uganda/kivengere_festo.htm/

Idi Amin
Wikipedia
http://en.wikipedia.org/wiki/Idi_Amin

Festo Kivengere
Wikipedia, http://en.wikipedia.org/wiki/Festo_Kivengere

Who is the Best Football Player in the World?
About.com African History
Biography of Idi Amin by Alistair Boddy-Evans
http://africanhistory.about.com/od/biography/a/bio_amin.htm

A wide range of Christian books is available from EP Books. If you would like a free catalogue please write to us or contact us by e-mail. Alternatively, you can view the whole catalogue online at our web sites.

EP BOOKS
Faverdale North
Darlington, DL3 0PH, England

www.epbooks.org
e-mail: sales@epbooks.org